Dear Sky

Letters from a *Sannyāsī*

Dear Sky

Letters from a *Sannyāsī*

Satsvarūpa dāsa Goswami

GN Press, Inc.

Persons interested in the subject matter of this book are invited to correspond with our secretary:

GN Press, Inc.
RD 1, Box 837-K
Port Royal, PA 17082

Printed in Port Royal, PA
United States of America
ISBN: 0-911233-99-7

Library of Congress Cataloging in Publication Data:

Goswami, Satsvarūpa Dāsa,
Dear Sky: Letters from a Sannyāsī / Satsvarūpa Dāsa Goswami.
p. cm.
ISBN 0-911233-99-7 : $10.00
1. Religious life—International Society for Krishna Consciousness. 2. Hindu meditations. 3. International Society for Krishna Consciousness—Doctrines. I. Title.
BL1285.852.G66 1993
294.5'512—dc20 93-28117
CIP

Contents

To Whom it May Concern:

I write about a hundred and fifty letters a month to devotees and friends around the Kṛṣṇa consciousness movement. But there are so many other things I would like to share in letters that never make it into my regular correspondence. Some of these things appear in this book.

The letters in the book are not constrained by formality or limited to an exchange that can only take place by sticking on a postage stamp and sealing an envelope. I have written to those to whom I felt inspired to speak at the moment, and sometimes those persons were as small as a backyard mushroom or as vast as the sky. A letter is meant to be a heart-to-heart exchange; that's what these letters are.

Our spiritual master, Śrīla Prabhupāda, has placed the order to preach on all of us, but he has especially stressed this order for his *sannyāsī* disciples. Preaching means sharing Kṛṣṇa consciousness with others, on a one-to-one basis, or with the entire world. This book is my small attempt to reach out to all those whom I have passed during this six-month period and either been too shy to approach, or too busy getting where I was supposed to be going, or for whatever reason, the moment wasn't right. These letters represent a second chance at giving them all some small taste of Kṛṣṇa's glories.

In addition to being a preacher, a *sannyāsī* is also a devotee and wants to be able to reveal his mind to confidential friends. Letters help serve that purpose. The letters I have written here come from actual experiences in my travels through half a year, although I have employed a fictive element in addressing the letters to many "people" to whom I normally wouldn't write. By the second half of the book, I had settled down in Wicklow, Ireland for a couple of weeks and my letters became focused on my friends—on all those whom I wanted to share Kṛṣṇa consciousness with. I hope that you, my friends, will find something useful here and will be inspired to share with me as I have tried to share with you.

Vaiṣṇava dāsānudāsa,

Satsvarupa das Goswami

Part One

February 16, 1992
Stroudsburg, Pennsylvania

Dear holy name,

Please accept my humble obeisances at your lotus feet. All glories to the pure devotees of Lord Caitanya who bring the names of Rādhā and Kṛṣṇa into this world.

I dare to address myself to You, Nāma Prabhu, only because I am under the direction of my spiritual master, His Divine Grace A.C. Bhaktivedanta Swami Prabhupāda. As stated in the *Caitanya-caritāmṛta, kṛṣṇa-śakti vinā nahe tāra pravartana,* unless a person is empowered directly by Kṛṣṇa, he cannot spread the holy names all over the world. Śrīla Prabhupāda has spread the glories of Kṛṣṇa's movement to every town and village, so I'm sure that Śrīla Prabhupāda is very dear to You. I am writing as one of his disciples.

Śrīla Prabhupāda brought the holy name into my heart and mind and put it on my tongue so that it might be my constant companion. He did this in the summer of 1966 when he began the International Society for Kṛṣṇa Consciousness in New York City. I was among the sorry-looking persons who came there out of the Lower East Side scene. I wasn't looking for the Swami or the Hare Kṛṣṇa mantra, but I am happy beyond any dream I might have for happiness with what I received from Śrīla Prabhupāda. Therefore I want to thank You, Holy Name, for appearing in my life. And I make it the aim of my life to try to please Śrīla

Prabhupāda by chanting and distributing this precious commodity of *hari-nāma,* either by encouraging people to chant privately *(japa),* or to take part in congregational chanting *(kīrtana).*

Śrīla Rūpa Gosvāmī writes, "The holy name, character, pastimes and activities of Kṛṣṇa are all transcendentally sweet like sugar candy. Although the tongue afflicted by the jaundice of *avidyā* (ignorance) cannot taste anything sweet, it is wonderful that simply by carefully chanting these sweet names every day, a natural relish awakens within his tongue, and his disease is gradually destroyed at the root." (Nectar of Instruction, text 7)

Lord Caitanya has described in His *Śikṣāṣṭakam* verse that when we begin to chant, we do not find the innate sweet taste which resides in the syllables of the Hare Kṛṣṇa mantra. He says we cannot taste the sweetness of the holy names because we commit offenses.

I am bereft of the sweet taste of the holy names. I don't like to speak of this before You because it may seem I am implying that You are not sweet or that You are not merciful. I don't mean that. I have faith in the purity and absolute nature of the holy name. But my faith is theoretical. I accept the injunction of the scriptures that the holy name is nondifferent from Kṛṣṇa and that if we chant carefully and devotedly, that realization of *kṛṣṇa-nāma* will arise in our hearts like the waxing moon. I also have faith that even the offensive or "shadow" chanting I am doing now will liberate me from the reactions of sins I have committed. But I am hankering for the realization of the holy name which leads to love of Kṛṣṇa.

When I thought of writing You, O Holy Name, my initial motive was to ask forgiveness for my offenses. I am perhaps afflicted with each of the ten offenses against the holy name, even though I don't always perceive that fact due to complacency. But the offense which I do perceive most clearly is the offense known as *pramāda*, inattention. Although each morning I chant as early as possible, and although I chant in a quiet place, my mind soon races away from the prize of attentive chanting and gives me instead a consciousness filled with plans, worries, and so many other distractions. Therefore, I don't chant the pure names of Kṛṣṇa *(śuddha-nāma)*. It is my desire that within this lifetime I may attain Your mercy so that I can chant with love.

I have heard from the reliable sources of guru, *śāstra*, and *sādhu*, that the first stage in chanting is to feel regret. I am not able to do this, but I hope the day will come when I realize with humility my fallen state and regret all the offenses I have committed to the holy name, to the devotees of the Lord, and to all other living entities. The state of sincere regret is a purifying stage, I know, and I have treasured the statements to this effect made by Bhaktivinoda Ṭhākura, Narottama dāsa Ṭhākura, and other Gauḍīya Vaiṣṇava *ācāryas*. And so I recite the words of Bhaktivinoda Ṭhākura: "When, oh, when will that day be mine? When, my offenses ceasing, taste for the holy name increasing, when in my heart will Your mercy shine? When, oh, when will that day be mine?"

O Holy Name, I hope to write to You again as I traverse this *bhakti-mārga.* In *Dear Sky,* I am writing many people, but I thought it best to start with a letter to my constant companion, the holy name. Please allow me to tell whomever I meet to chant Hare Kṛṣṇa. And if You give me a drop of mercy for chanting *śuddha-nāma,* then I will be enthusiastic to pass that on to others.

February 17
Stroudsburg, PA

Dear day, February 17, 1992,

Our spiritual master, Śrīla Prabhupāda, once said that a particular day, March 2, 1973, will never come again. Time moves on, and you too will be gone, just like a cloud moving across the sky.

Day, you are given to me by Kṛṣṇa. I bow down to you. I embrace you. I have you for just a little while and then you will leave me. I can make the most of your presence in my life or I can waste you.

Speaking in the mood of Rādhārāṇī and the *gopīs,* Lord Caitanya said that if ever He got the chance to be with Kṛṣṇa again, He would worship the minutes and the hours of that time. He would offer *ārati* to the moments; He would decorate them. That time in which we can meet Kṛṣṇa or become Kṛṣṇa conscious is very precious. We worship that time.

I wish I could attain Kṛṣṇa consciousness today, February 17, 1992.

Every Sunday here in Stroudsburg, I remark to Śamīka Ṛṣi Prabhu, "Well, now it's another Sunday. What will you do today?" It seems that only a minute goes by and I'm saying it again, "Now it's Sunday." A week goes by so fast, and a month, and a year. But still this day is here. This precious day.

As you fly by, I salute you. Now you will go, to wherever past days go, and you will gather with the rest. Since you are an expansion of Kṛṣṇa—*kāla*—maybe I will meet with you when I become spiritually fit and free of time's shackles. Maybe I'll meet with you in the spiritual world in spiritual time where we're not bothered by past, present, and future. What that is like I don't know. Probably my urge to speak to you and to love you is a shadow of my desire to enter into that spiritual day where early morning means going to make arrangements for the pastimes of Rādhā and Kṛṣṇa. It's that day that I want to see. And you, February 17, 1992, are it's representative. You are a little spot on the *bhakti-mārga*. By Prabhupāda's grace, this day is not wasted, but engaged in Kṛṣṇa's service.

Thank you for being. As you leave, please remember me to Kṛṣṇa.

February 18
Stroudsburg, PA

Dear critical Godbrother,

Please accept my humble obeisances.

I heard a friend of mine told you I'm starting to write *Dear Sky.* (I wish he hadn't leaked that information because I've only begun these letters, and I'm afraid my enthusiasm may get nipped in the bud.) Your question is whether I'm going to write any letters to women. You have a general concern: "If a *sannyāsī* writes letters to women, isn't that breaking the principles of *sannyāsa*?"

Ironically, just the other day I was challenged with the opposite question. It came from an old friend from my college days. He said, "I heard you're starting to write a book of letters from a *sannyāsī*. I hope you're going to include some love letters to women. But probably you're not. Don't you think that limits your humanity?"

I told him that a *sannyāsī* doesn't write love letters to women, but that's not limiting to his humanity. I explained some of the principles of celibacy, but I doubt whether it got through to him. He thinks that if a person gives up sex, it must be because of some psychological hang up.

I explained to my friend that there have been celibates, both men and women, throughout history, who decided they wanted to give everything to God. We can also go on loving people even while we're celibate. I told him that I know what sex is and I also know why I didn't get full satisfaction from it. No one can get full satisfaction from physical sex. It's not meant to give that. It is given to us by Nature for the purposes of procreation.

I don't think my friend will hear me with faith. It's so difficult to communicate with nondevotees.

But it's different speaking to you. I'm surprised that you are in doubt whether a *sannyāsī* can give any guidance to women devotees. That seems to be the implication of your question. Now let me ask you a question: "How are women going to get guidance when they come to spiritual life?"

If you ask me whether it's risky, I would have to say yes. We can form attachments. Even if it doesn't lead to a physical falldown, it can be a burden on the mind and turn into a subtle falldown.

But the spiritual masters in our *sampradāya* have traditionally accepted women disciples. If one feels that it's going to be a grave problem, he should not accept women disciples. Certainly the risk comes under the same category as not accepting too many disciples. This injunction is given because the burden of the disciples' karma, whether they are male or female, can weaken the one giving initiation. But Śrīla Prabhupāda writes in *The Nectar of Devotion* that if one keeps preaching and follows the principles strictly, he will not fall down. Moreover, he will be pleasing to Kṛṣṇa for trying to increase the number of devotees.

There are some basic injunctions for *sannyāsa* life. If we follow them, they will protect us. A *san-*

nyāsī doesn't associate intimately with women. Prabhupāda told the story of Bhaktisiddhānta Sarasvatī Ṭhākura who refused to meet alone with a young woman. The lady was young enough to be his granddaughter or even his great granddaughter. In the presence of her husband, she asked Bhaktisiddhānta Sarasvatī Ṭhākura for a private meeting. He said, "No, I cannot talk with you alone. Whatever you want to say, you can say here." That is the *sannyāsa* standard—not to meet with women alone.

Private phone conversations are also a kind of solitary exchange, I would agree. And letter exchanges, in one sense, are about as private as you can get. All I can say is that I'm aware of the dangers of misuse, and I will always try to avoid them. I don't want to become someone's shadow husband or shadow paramour. I don't want to become a hypocrite. If I see, even in a subtle, small way, that any of these improprieties are creeping into my relationships—even through the mail—I will tear them out like weeds in the garden.

I think it's helpful if a *sannyāsī* travels frequently so he doesn't get attached to any particular set of disciples and doesn't accept steady service from any particular women or stay with them in close quarters. He can periodically cleanse away entangling cobwebs by association with renounced Vaiṣṇavas if he is fortunate enough to find them. And by performing his austerities with duty and devotion, he will free himself from accumulating attachments.

But in the name of sparing ourselves burdens, I don't think we can go to the extreme of vanquishing women or refusing to write them. Sooner or later, one has to actually become a spiritual father and stop looking upon others as victims for sense gratification. We have to see the sincerity of spirit-souls, whether embodied as men or women, and encourage their good qualities.

February 20
Stroudsburg, PA

Dear icy trees,

You look so beautiful this morning. It's been raining all night. The temperature is just at freezing, so ice has formed on your boughs. Although you look beautiful, I know you're cold. Still, Kṛṣṇa makes everything so beautiful. I'm not on the Vṛndāvana standard, and perhaps you trees are not either. I can't talk with you and say, "Have you seen the son of Mahārāja Nanda? You appear to have turned white in bliss and are shivering in ecstasy due to His touch."

I can't talk like that unless I pretend. These trees are in the mode of ignorance (if they don't mind my saying so); Prabhupāda said any living entity can benefit if we chant Hare Kṛṣṇa Hare Kṛṣṇa, Kṛṣṇa Kṛṣṇa Hare Hare/Hare Rāma Hare Rāma, Rāma Rāma Hare Hare. Even these trees.

Icy trees, I had the urge to reach out to you, but then I thought, "What is this, Nature worship?" I recall Prabhupāda telling the devotees when they remarked how beautiful the sunset was, that we are not interested in the sunrise or the sunset, we are interested in the creator of the sunrise and the sunset. Prabhupāda's statement doesn't negate the beauty of the sun or the shimmering icy trees or the bright gray sky of dawn on a cloudy day, but it means we shouldn't forget the source of this beauty. His land is a million times more beautiful than this world. We shouldn't become enamored by this place.

We are in a bad situation. We have this bodily identification. We're headed for *saṁsāra.* We think we are the center of the universe. It's all wrong. We're trying to adjust to these conditions without making the real solution to surrender to God. In the midst of this wrongness, to see some beauty in nature is not sufficient to save us. It's just a tiny, tiny spark of God consciousness. It can even be another form of defiance of God. But to see the beauty in terms of Kṛṣṇa is another thing. That can be glorification of Kṛṣṇa and remembrance of Him.

Therefore I offer my obeisances to Kṛṣṇa, the original Creator, and hope that by transcendental loving service we can come to see Him in a land which is never created out of the mode of passion, but which eternally exists in the *sandhinī* potency of the Lord. His creation is not a puzzle or a riddle or a place of ignorance, but it is enlightened with the *saṁvit* potency of the Lord. His creation is a place where all living entities, including trees, are filled with the *ānanda* or the *hlādinī-śakti* potency of serving Śrīmatī Rādhārāṇī in Her pastimes with the Supreme Lord, Kṛṣṇa.

Do you hear what I'm saying, trees? Does it penetrate your covering and reach your soul? Let me not tease you or be condescending toward you just because I'm in a human body. If you can hear my words, then you can also hear the sound vibration of Hare Kṛṣṇa Hare Kṛṣṇa. I'm no better than you are, but I am able to vibrate these sounds as I've heard from my spiritual master. I can recite them with the faith he has given me. One devotee, Prahlāda Mahārāja, said to his demon friends who, like you, were also in the mode of ignorance: "I'm speaking on the faith of my spiritual master, and if you hear me with that faith, you can also become a *bhakta*." So I'm raising my voice a little louder because you may be slightly deaf due to your bodily covering. If I can serve you by giving you the holy names, then that is bliss. Hare Kṛṣṇa Hare Kṛṣṇa, Kṛṣṇa Kṛṣṇa Hare Hare/Hare Rāma Hare Rāma, Rāma Rāma Hare Hare. Hear Hare Kṛṣṇa and echo it back in your own *kīrtana*. Wait for the day when Kṛṣṇa will deliver you. Kṛṣṇa personally delivered the twin Arjuna trees. He can deliver all of us if we simply regret our wrongs and pray to desire to be happy in our constitutional position serving Kṛṣṇa.

February 21
Stroudsburg, PA

To the people who live on Brislin Road,

On my morning walks past your houses, I see your children lining up to catch the school bus. You go outside to dote on them as I come by. Sometimes you eye me strangely because I'm something new on your block and because I'm not going off to work or school like everybody else. What do I actually do when I turn the corner and walk into the woods every morning?

Normally I love to sing as I walk—the "Gurv-aṣṭakam" prayers or the Hare Kṛṣṇa mantra. But when I walk by your houses I fall silent. I guess I feel a little uneasy about the fact that I'm so different from you.

Once I reach the woods, I'm able to sing. And sometimes I talk out loud to myself, making plans for books I want to write or how to improve my chanting. I know this is no concern to you in your houses, but I wanted to tell you that I'm a happy man.

What makes me happy? The fact that I sing Hare Kṛṣṇa and I'm a devotee in Kṛṣṇa consciousness.

The happiness I feel comes in being cleansed in heart by the giving up of sinful activities. To become free from sin, you first have to get knowledge, and that comes by associating with knowledgeable persons. They are rare in this world. By God's grace, I met a pure devotee of Kṛṣṇa, His Divine Grace A.C. Bhaktivedanta Swami Prabhupāda. He taught me that love of God is the source of true happiness. He transformed my life for the better. This makes me so happy that I like to sing about it.

Prabhupāda taught me about the Supreme Personality of Godhead, Kṛṣṇa. When I hear about Kṛṣṇa's beautiful form and His blissful devotees and the playful and loving ways they associate together in the spiritual world, I feel a happiness that's beyond anything in this material world. I wish I could share some of this with you, but I don't know how to bridge the gap between us. You see what I'm doing as a form of Indian religion. You're puzzled why an American should follow it. I want to suggest that you wholeheartedly embrace whatever religion you follow. Jesus Christ also taught that love of God brings happiness to the self and is not dependent on wealth or position in this material world.

I've said hello and I feel better for it. I wanted to get free of the intimidation I have when I walk past your homes or when we exchange looks. So I'm saying "hello" and best wishes. Maybe when we meet again, we can exchange smiles. We have nothing to lose.

February 22
Stroudsburg, PA

Dear Kṛṣṇa, my *caitya-guru,*

Dear Lord, I thought of speaking to You today because I finished writing another book. I am happy about that. I know there are faults in the book, but still, it was by Your mercy that I was able to pass on the instructions of the spiritual masters and scriptures. I'm thanking You because I know at any moment my intelligence might be removed, leaving me unable to think or write a word. I'm speaking in gratefulness on this occasion.

As I finished work on my newest manuscript, I made a prayer that I could continue to write or to serve the devotees in any way that You desire. I wish to be guided in the way best suited for coming as quickly as possible to Your lotus feet. You are very kind, Kṛṣṇa, and very lenient. You allow us to do what we want, and You give us the sanction, but at the same time You tell us what's best for us. Sometimes what's best is not what we're doing.

For most conditioned souls this duality becomes extreme—I mean the difference between what we're doing and what You want us to do. But still, You leniently allow us to do what we want, although we have to face the results in terms of our karma.

I was in the worst situation, living in my imagination and against the laws of God. But Prabhupāda picked me up and put me in tune with the wishes of Kṛṣṇa. Now I chant Your holy names and follow the regulative principles on the *bhakti-mārga*. But still, I know that I do things my way, which is not always Your way. Therefore I pray, "Please give me the intelligence and the courage to do what You want me to do."

Dear Lord, I'm writing this letter on the appearance day of Bhaktisiddhānta Sarasvatī Ṭhākura. I wish to thank You for sending him to this world. He so strongly presented the teachings of Rūpa Gosvāmī and laid down the foundation (which he received from his father, Bhaktivinoda Ṭhākura) for worldwide Kṛṣṇa consciousness. He also gave instructions to our Śrīla Prabhupāda to preach to English-speaking people. That is how the worldwide Kṛṣṇa consciousness movement began. I'm grateful to the glorious teacher, Bhaktisiddhānta Sarasvatī Ṭhākura, for instructing our Śrīla Prabhupāda to come to us. Prabhupāda considered himself the humble servant of his Guru Mahārāja. His Guru Mahārāja's teachings were his life's breath. Prabhupāda was an ideal disciple. At every step he served his spiritual master. So the ideal of what I'm asking You, dear *caitya-guru,* is already before me in the example of my spiritual master, who followed Śrīla Bhaktisiddhānta Sarasvatī Ṭhākura with full faith. Our Prabhupāda said, "I have no special qualification. I'm not a magician of mystic powers. I'm not a great scholar or a great devotee. But I have full faith in my spiritual master, and I carry out his order. That's all." Ah, what a great qualification! To be selfless! Prabhupāda was like that.

The years are quickly going by for me. I'm one of the oldest devotees in ISKCON, but that seniority has become a source of shame. I'm not molding myself intensely—as our Śrīla Prabhupāda did—to completely carrying out the desires of my spiritual master. So I'm writing this letter to place myself before You. I am the little bird on the tree who is tasting the bitter and sweet fruits, and You are the witness and observer. Please give me a hint. Please give me a signal so that I can turn to You in earnestness and give up everything except what You want me to do. I don't want to waste time. Bhaktisiddhānta Sarasvatī Ṭhākura said we should finish up our business in this life and go back to Godhead.

I understand that to serve Rādhā-Kṛṣṇa in Vṛndāvana is only rarely attained; even demigods like Brahmā and Śiva cannot attain it. I cannot expect to go there quickly, but I'm praying to have fixed in my mind and heart before this life is over, a definite conclusion *(bhāva-mayī)* of what I want to be.

All glories to the Supersoul who accompanies the aspiring *bhaktas* on the path of pure devotional service! Please Lord, destroy the darkness of ignorance in me with the torchlight of Your knowledge. Let me serve Śrīla Prabhupāda and all the Vaiṣṇavas. Please always be my friend to whom I can turn in difficulty, in joy, in boredom. You are God. I can always converse with You, and You have so kindly come into my heart. Let me never forget that the Supreme Master is with me, protecting me, receiving my service, and seeing what nonsense I do. With this in mind, let me try to be a better devotee.

February 23
Stroudsburg, PA

Dear Śrīla Jīva Gosvāmī Prabhupāda,

Please accept my humble *daṇḍavats* in the dust of your lotus feet. All glories to Gurudeva and Gaurāṅga.

I know I am being presumptuous to write to such a great *ācārya* as yourself. It's one thing for me to write to His Divine Grace A.C. Bhaktivedanta Swami Prabhupāda, because he lifted me out of *māyā* and made me a devotee. But Prabhupāda has said that the six Gosvāmīs are our *śikṣā-gurus* and that we may worship you by reading your books.

Although I can't understand philosophy very well (being an example of Kali-yuga, dull intelligence) I hear your teachings regularly. Your *Sandarbhas* have been re-spoken in the teachings and writings of Bhaktisiddhānta Sarasvatī Ṭhākura, and my own Śrīla Prabhupāda is his disciple.

I'm writing in appreciation. Last night, my friend Madhu and I read *Saṅkalpa-kalpa-drumaḥ* and enjoyed hearing Kṛṣṇa's pastimes from you. I think of you more as a philosopher than a *rasācārya* like Rūpa Gosvāmī or Viśvanātha Cakravartī. But I know that you, Śrīla Jīva Gosvāmī Prabhupāda, are also full of the nectar of Kṛṣṇa consciousness. You always give us the conclusions of Kṛṣṇa consciousness according to the scriptures, and Kṛṣṇa's pastimes are revealed to you in your heart.

May I recite for your pleasure a few of the things that I particularly liked in your book? Sometimes in the verses you refer to Kṛṣṇa as "your beloved Kṛṣṇa." We know that Kṛṣṇa is the beloved of Rādhārāṇī and all the residents of Vṛndāvana, but in some verses, you include us, the readers of *kṛṣṇa-kathā,* and tell us about "your Kṛṣṇa." Thank you for including us in that way.

You said in one verse, "O Kṛṣṇa, as the king and queen of Vraja daily meditated on You, so we have given these pictures of You. We have not invented anything." (2.64) I thought, "Yes, that is Jīva Gosvāmī assuring us that what he has given is in no way concocted." I know you do this so that devotees who come after you, like ourselves, can defeat doubters and show that everything about Kṛṣṇa is true reality, backed by authoritative Vedic references.

I like the sweet exchanges you describe between Mother Yaśodā and Kṛṣṇa, such as when she asked if she could come into the forest every day and cook for Him there. You have also given us some sweet verses on Śrīmatī Rādhārāṇī pining away during the hours when Kṛṣṇa is in the forest and She has to stay at home. Here are some of those verses:

> With Her friends' help She made a garland for Lord Kṛṣṇa. Although She spent the time singing peerless sweet songs about Lord Kṛṣṇa's glories, She could find no peace.
>
> She wore musk *tilaka,* sapphire earrings, and garments like a monsoon cloud. Her complexion was like Lord Kṛṣṇa's yellow garments. She burned with love for Kṛṣṇa.

You describe how Śrīmatī Rādhārāṇī asked one of the eunuch guards in Her house to go to Kṛṣṇa's palace, find out what He was doing, and come back to tell Her. We have a nice narration by the guard, with many details of Kṛṣṇa milking the cows, taking sweet rice for breakfast, joking and playing. Thank you for giving us all this nectar.

This morning when I thought of writing a letter to someone, your name came to mind spontaneously. I hesitated because you are such a grave personality. But then I thought, "If I decide I can't write to Jīva Gosvāmī, then neither can I write to Rūpa Gosvāmī, or Raghunātha dāsa Gosvāmī, or Gopāla Bhaṭṭa, or Raghunātha Bhaṭṭa, or Viśvanātha Cakravartī, or any past *ācārya*. Then I certainly can't write to Kṛṣṇa Himself." Therefore, I decided not to waver but to write to the person who inspired me by his book, Śrīla Jīva Gosvāmī Prabhupāda. Please, therefore, forgive me for this presumptuousness. It is done out of affection and a desire to worship your lotus feet. I wish to be a follower of the six Gosvāmīs by following Śrīla Prabhupāda and serving in ISKCON.

Although I'm talking childishly, I know that there is a serious link between us. We are in one spiritual family as followers of Śrī Caitanya Mahāprabhu. All you great souls, who exist simultaneously in your *nitya-līlā* as *mañjarīs* with Rādhārāṇī and as pure devotees in Caitanya-līlā, are always experiencing the greatest bliss. We wish to add to your bliss, if possible, by giving you the satisfaction of seeing that the works you left in this material world are not being neglected. They are not being secretly kept by a few *bābājīs* in India. Neither are your works slowly rotting away on palm leaves nor being destroyed by poor people who use them for fuel. Your works have been translated, reprinted, and repeated in essence through *ācāryas* like Bhaktisiddhānta Sarasvatī and our Śrīla Prabhupāda. As a result, we can all be strong in Kṛṣṇa consciousness. Every day we use your examples as part of our regular preaching.

I make repeated *daṇḍavats* to you and all of the six Gosvāmīs. I hope that you will allow me to speak to you on occasion. I will remind my friends that we may all approach our spiritual predecessors and that you accept our service and wish to bring us up to the standard of pure Kṛṣṇa consciousness. Thank you very much.

February 24
Stroudsburg, PA

Dear moon,

Please accept my obeisances.

You look rather mysterious in the sky today. It's turning light, and you're just about to disappear from our vision. I know that you're always there. It's just the shifting of the planet that keeps us from seeing you. But still, to see you in your last moments—a half moon, white and pale. Just a half moon, half covered. So mysterious. Even as I look, filmy clouds obscure the half of you that we can just see—and then a moment later, you are peeking out again.

You are one of Kṛṣṇa's eyes. You saw the *rāsa* dance. Kṛṣṇa came and performed His *aprākṛta* Goloka activities on the same planet where we work and live. There's a line in Jayadeva Gosvāmī's *Gīta-govinda* stating that the moon was astonished to see the *rāsa* dance. I think of that now when I look up at you. The moon is a planet. Demigods live there. The whole big planet was looking down at the *rāsa* dance.

Ah! There you are again. Now all we can see is one little pie slice. It seems like you have moved to a different part of the sky, lower down, and are more deeply shrouded in clouds. I'm keeping my eye on you so that I can write you this letter.

You give me an occasion to talk about Kṛṣṇa. And I can relate to you, because as you were far,

far away from the *rāsa* dance, I'm far, far away too. I can only see it from a distance, if at all. We get a glimpse of the *rāsa* dance in some of the paintings showing the innocence and playfulness of Kṛṣṇa and the *gopīs*. The boys and girls are dancing in the open meadow. Kṛṣṇa has expanded Himself to dance beside each *gopī*. It's the middle of the night, but you, dear moon, have filled the sky with light. You can become so bright that Rādhārāṇī is afraid Her relatives will see Her go to meet Kṛṣṇa in the evening. Therefore, Śrīmatī Rādhikā covers all the parts of Her body with white cloth; even Her hands are covered with white flowers. She is trying to blend in with the overall lightness. That's the effect you have, moon.

I look up and see you looking pale. Your mouth is open and you appear to be lamenting. I am also lamenting. I wish I could chant Hare Kṛṣṇa better. It's human to turn to someone who seems sympathetic, so I choose you, moon, as a person to whom I can speak in a confidential mood.

In transcendental madness the *gopīs* speak to all living beings. But those living beings are actually the sentient and intelligent creatures of Vṛndāvana. I don't claim divine madness, but I am attracted to talking to you, an old friend I have known all my life. I want to compliment you on having seen the *rāsa* dance. It's better than I have done. You are old, but still you look graceful and pale in the morning. As the eye of the Lord, you can also see me. Maybe if I speak to you, Kṛṣṇa will also hear me. In this world, there are so many unfriendly people. Even devotees are sometimes hard to approach. It's nice to be able to talk to the silent moon on a cold, clear, winter morning.

February 25
Stroudsburg, PA

Dear devotees in Vṛndāvana,

Please accept my humble obeisances. All glories to Śrīla Prabhupāda.

It's hailing where I am, and I'm out walking. Ice is bouncing off my bulky winter coat. I imagine it's cold in Vṛndāvana too, but not like this! When I finish this walk, I can go into a warm house, but you are always in the cold. You're in *tapa-bhūmi.* But of course you have something incomparable—you live in Vṛndāvana, Kṛṣṇa's abode. The most I have here is that I can think of Vṛndāvana. I'm thinking of the place where you live.

One reason I'm writing is to remind you of your fortune. Please never take it for granted that you live in Vṛndāvana-*dhāma.*

I'm just a tourist, but when I do go back to Vṛndāvana I would like to go on *parikrama,* make obeisances, and pray to become the servant of Rādhārāṇī. I also think of being with those friends with whom I can share these thoughts.

I'm looking forward to being with you to talk about chanting. Sometimes I'm embarrassed to admit that I don't have so many other interests in the Kṛṣṇa consciousness movement. I don't even want many duties other than the duties of chanting and hearing. If I can become proficient in these things, I can be a good counselor and a good devotee in other ways. For me, these are the important things, and I know they're important for you too.

Is there any way I can help you? Anything I can get you? I'll send you some things as soon as I find someone going to India. So let me know what I should send. I already know you like olive oil, Pilot pens, and batteries.

And you know what I'm looking for. I'm always eager for words from our favorite *sādhus* and news of Krishna-Balaram Mandir and yourselves. How are you practicing Kṛṣṇa consciousness?

Me and some of the *brahmacārīs* here have been reading from the six Gosvāmīs' literature in the evenings. Last night we read from Jīva Gosvāmī's *Saṅkalpa-kalpa-drumaḥ.* In one verse he glorifies the inner Vṛndāvana, which he says is not perceivable in the outer Vṛndāvana:

> Within the realm of Vṛndāvana manifested on the earth, an unmanifested realm of Vṛndāvana, invisible to ordinary eyes, exists. In that invisible realm Lord Kṛṣṇa eternally enjoys blissful pastimes with the people of Vraja.
>
> —*Saṅkalpa-kalpa-drumaḥ,* 2.1

You have a better chance of contacting the inner Vṛndāvana because you're so close to it. You can see Govardhana and the Yamunā. The local people will say "Jaya Rādhe!" in passing. You are in the place where Kṛṣṇa appeared, so the clues are certainly more evident than here in the hail-storming suburbs of Pennsylvania.

Thinking of you and Vṛndāvana gives me a nice feeling of separation. Thank you for receiving this letter because it allowed me to enter the mood I desired. Don't feel obliged to answer me at length, but at least a few lines in an aerogram . . . And if you're inclined, you can tell me what it's like to live in Vṛndāvana.

March 3
Long Island, New York

Dear death,

I call you death, but I don't mean Yamarāja.

Recently a devotee wrote me a letter and asked me many intricate questions about Yamarāja. I said I didn't know the answers. He wanted to know if Yamarāja only treats sinful persons and Kṛṣṇa treats the others. And, who judges persons who are not demons, but not devotees? I replied that all I knew was what I had read in the Sixth Canto. Yamarāja tells his messengers that they should leave the devotees alone and only go after people who are averse to the lotus feet of Kṛṣṇa. I owned up and said I can only answer simple questions, but I have faith that everything happens by Kṛṣṇa's arrangement. I don't know how my food is digested, how many hairs I have on my head, and how the leaves sprout green in the spring. I don't know practically anything, but I know everything is happening by Kṛṣṇa's arrangement. However, Kṛṣṇa does clearly say that Yamarāja does not come for the devotees.

Then what kind of death do we contemplate as *sādhakas?* If Kṛṣṇa does not take us on a chariot to Vaikuṇṭha (or to Vraja) at the end of this life because we're not yet pure, how do we get to the next place? And who takes us? I don't think this detail is so important. But still the question remains: who am I talking about when I say, "Dear death"?

It's a fact I'm thinking of you, Death. Thinking about death brings anxiety. We have our present plans and they may extend as far as a year or two into the future. Sometimes we even dare to plan further ahead. If we do think about death, we usually plan to have warning and then go to Vṛndāvana to spend our last six months. But it may not be like that at all. The next time I go downstairs to the bathroom, it may be all over, even while I'm not thinking the final thoughts I've planned to think, even while my chanting is poor. It's that fear that you, dear death, may come at an unexpected time, especially in an awkward place where there are no devotees, or before I am prepared.

Prabhupāda tells us that death comes to a devotee like a cat who picks up her kittens. The cat takes the kittens in her mouth, holding them gently by the skin on their necks. It doesn't hurt the kittens; for them it is a pleasure. But when death comes for the nondevotee or sinful man, it's like the cat who catches the rat by the throat.

We know that we will be helpless at the time of death; we will not be in control. We will try to think of Kṛṣṇa, and then death will handle us accordingly. So death, you have your own date with me. I can't say I'm waiting for you eagerly. I do love this life of travel and writing, and I am eager to spend more of this lifetime hearing from the *ācāryas* and reading about Rādhā and Kṛṣṇa. I'm just beginning.

I'm on the verge of asking you to please give me more time, but I should not pray like that. My prayer is to the all-living, eternal, blissful Kṛṣṇa and His *pariṣad*. My prayer is to Śrīla Prabhupāda: "Please prepare me for death by allowing me to live life as fully as possible in surrender to you."

If there's anything we wish of death, I suppose we wish that it not be so shocking or fearful or abrupt that it affects our consciousness for the next life. But even that is not something we have to worry about too much. As Prabhupāda once said to the wife of an epileptic devotee, even if he died in a fit and was apparently forgetful, Kṛṣṇa would not hold it against him. Up until the point where one is no longer conscious and competent in mind, Kṛṣṇa accepts our last loving thoughts. We have nothing to fear from death.

But still we fear. Let it be an impetus, then, not to waste time and to pray to Kṛṣṇa: "Please engage me in Your service. Please let me chant the holy names." Before death takes us, we must be fully Kṛṣṇa conscious.

March 6
Santa Domingo, Dominican Republic

Dear old lady looking in the window,

I was surprised to see you standing by the barred window. Do you remember the moment? I was the Hare Kṛṣṇa devotee who had come from America and the devotees at the Santa Domingo temple were having a reception for me. I was sitting on a chair in the front hall—they were having *kīrtana* and performing *ārati,* and you were looking in the window. I was surprised to see you. Your face was so very, very old, completely wrinkled, and although your mouth was closed, I could tell you were toothless.

The thought flashed through my mind that you were once a young woman, but now you're so old that you're not pleasant to look at. You yourself must be aware that you're at the very end of your existence. It's so plain to see that your body is reduced to nothing and nearly finished, like an old fruit or an old flower. You are a walking reminder to everybody of what's going to happen to them.

I remember you. When the foot-bathing ceremony was over, and the lecture was over, and the cheers were over, my impression of you was as strong as of everything else. You seemed curious about what was going on, and I wonder what your impression of us was.

I don't know whether you were able to hear the translation of the speech. I was telling the devotees how fortunate we are to have received the

Hare Kṛṣṇa mantra and to be able to live in Prabhupāda's shelter. That blessing could extend to you also, even at the fag end of your life. Any person, old or young, can come to Kṛṣṇa consciousness. I know that just by hearing Hare Kṛṣṇa it was good for you, and I hope that somehow you can embrace the chanting of Hare Kṛṣṇa. Then in your next life you can be happy in Kṛṣṇa consciousness. Each one of us, as we come to that toothless, shriveled-up stage, should count our blessings that we can hear from Prabhupāda, whether from inside the temple or by standing outside looking in. All glories to Prabhupāda. All glories to the Hare Kṛṣṇa mantra.

March 7
Santa Domingo

To the people of Santa Domingo
hearing *harināma,*

I'm the shaven-headed, white-bodied devotee from the U.S. who was playing the *karatālas* with the *harināma* party. After the *kīrtana,* a Dominican devotee spoke to you in Spanish. I was only able to pick up a word or two of what he was saying. He seemed to talk quite a bit about Christianity and Jesus and about how the chanting was universal and not sectarian, but I can't say for sure. Anyway, I wanted to speak to you, but since I don't speak Spanish, I decided to write you a letter.

Every devotee-visitor who comes here has the same impression of those of you who gather around our *harināma* party. You are nice people. I didn't see a single angry face in the whole crowd of two hundred people. You are simple and down-to-earth.

I want to thank you for listening to our chanting. Please take a plate of *halavā* when it's passed around to you. It's free, and even though there's not much of it, I think you'll like the taste. It has been offered to Kṛṣṇa, to God. It is holy.

There are many things that we Hare Kṛṣṇa people have learned from our spiritual master that are helpful for anyone who wants to love God. Most of these things don't take much effort to perform, yet they are beneficial. For example, the offering of food. God gives us everything that we eat. If we first offer it to Him with devotion, He accepts it from us. When He eats He does so in a spiritual way simply by hearing our prayers, and He leaves the food for our nourishment. Then it's no longer food, but *prasādam*, the remnants of food taken by Kṛṣṇa. Isn't it wonderful? Why don't you try it? We can teach you some beautiful prayers to say when you offer your food.

I hope the Dominican devotees will be able to communicate with you more directly. You can visit our temple and restaurant and come to our programs. You can join in the chanting of Hare Kṛṣṇa Hare Kṛṣṇa, Kṛṣṇa Kṛṣṇa Hare Hare/Hare Rāma Hare Rāma, Rāma Rāma Hare Hare.

I saw you, man with a military hat and those bloody-looking scratch marks on your arm. They looked like somebody practicing to make tattoos. You were a ragged-looking fellow, but you were smiling to hear our *kīrtana*. And you were glad to accept *prasādam*. Even those men I saw joking with one of the devotees at the book table seemed to be having a warm exchange. It's just amazing how you people are so receptive to the chanting and to the devotees.

It was about six o'clock on a Saturday. You didn't seem in a hurry to go elsewhere, but stopped and listened to the chanting—so many of you! Yes, I mean you in the sexy T-shirts, and you in the Adidas T-shirts, and you in the Indiana 1987 Basketball Champs T-shirts; dark-skinned, light-skinned, young and old—all of you. I thank you on behalf of the devotees for stopping to listen. Now let's get back to more chanting. Please join us.

March 8
Santa Domingo

Dear sky,

I came up to the roof to address Kṛṣṇa, or just to talk out loud. Different people and projects may engage us, but when we take away the trappings, we want to stand on a roof under the sky and say, "Kṛṣṇa, please help me. I want to talk, and I want to enjoy, and I want to sleep—so many things. I just go through life like that, but what I really want is You."

That's why I came to this roof. There are many pairs of shoes and sleeping bags up here because devotees sleep here during the night. I'm aware of their presence, although right now I'm alone. And although it's only 6:25 A.M., cars are starting to go by and the beautiful sky is turning light. O Kṛṣṇa, O Rādhā, I wish that I could see at least a part of You in Nature—the sky, the grayish sky. The pastimes of Kṛṣṇa, the sky in Vṛndāvana. Let us be reminded of You. And for that we want to go alone, because alone we can speak to that part of us, that isolated part, which yearns for Kṛṣṇa, which is not affected by the daily activities of our life. Kṛṣṇa, may that part of me thrive and grow so that I can think only of Your pastimes.

I came to confess, Kṛṣṇa. My chanting is so sleepy, so poor. I don't know what Hare Kṛṣṇa is, but somehow when I come up here it becomes clear that I do wish I could be Your devotee, to be with You and talk with You and serve You with the other *vrajavāsīs.* Therefore I thank You, and I thank you, sky. If I come back later, you won't be the same. Your pale colors will have disappeared along with this opportunity. But I'll try to come again and I'll try to retain some of this moment. Hare Kṛṣṇa.

March 9
Santa Domingo

Dear secret self,

Last night I thought again about being on the roof at dawn and the letter I wrote there. The thought came while Madhu and I were reading about a scene that takes place just before sunrise. The birds, the roosters, and all of Vṛndā-devī's creatures are trying to wake Rādhā and Kṛṣṇa so They can go home before Their parents find Them missing. The dawn is beautifully compared to a girl in a crimson *sarī* with *kuṅkuma* on her face.

Even here in mundane Santa Domingo it's the same earth planet; it's the same sun starting to redden on the eastern horizon. And there's also a rooster crowing, although I know he's not directly inspired by Vṛndā-devī.

(These topics are confidential, so I hesitate to relate it in a letter. Devotees have told me that some feelings are better not shared with everyone. It may be said that some feelings are not even to be put into words. I agree on principle, but the attempt to find expression is not outside our philosophy. The *ācāryas* readily admit that they cannot fully express Kṛṣṇa's beauty and the feelings of *rasa*, but they make an attempt to do so. They try by their beautiful poetry to give us some idea what the Absolute Beauty is. Even a person who is unqualified may be encouraged to express something about Kṛṣṇa, because even inadequate descriptions can create a revolution in the impious civilization.)

Quickly the sky lightens. Rādhā and Kṛṣṇa linger in Their pastimes, not listening to the warnings of the birds that they should go home at once. Finally Vṛndā-devī signals to the old monkey in the tree. She screeches, J-a-ṭ-i-l-ā! Jaṭilā is coming! Rādhā and Kṛṣṇa and the *gopīs* become frightened and run home. That scene of Them running together hand in hand into Vraja village, and, at a certain point, breaking apart—one going to Nandagrām, one to Yāvaṭ—is wonderful.

Perhaps a little *sūtra* form of that Vṛndāvana dawn can be kept in our hearts. Then when we see the early morning sky, we can remember that there is something special and hidden from everyone's eyes and thoughts which is the actual meaning of dawn. At least we have heard it, so we will not see dawn in the same way again. We don't see dawn as the time when the school bus driver gets in his bus and drives to his post. We don't see dawn as the stale leftovers of sense gratifiers spewing out of the clubs after a night of sinful activity. We don't see dawn as the time when a line of headlights moves down the highway toward another day's work.

This is our secret, and we hanker to return to Vṛndāvana in India to draw closer to this wonderful thing that is hidden from us. We want to walk out to the grove and chant Hare Kṛṣṇa as the sky lightens. There, the songs and activities of the birds reflect the pastimes of Rādhā and Kṛṣṇa. All creatures come forth to wake the Lord.

March 11
Puerto Rico

Dear friends,

Tonight I meet with a group of disciples. I'll sit in a chair. I have no prepared script or text to read from, but I will probably pick out a paragraph from the *Caitanya-caritāmṛta, Ādi-līlā* about the need for a guru. The definition of guru is given there: he is not the enjoyer of facilities supplied by the disciples, but is a humble servant of the Lord; he is to be seen by the disciples as the representative of Kṛṣṇa. I will throw out some of these ideas and see if there are any questions. I know there are a few disciples living in this area who have rejected me in favor of the philosophy that they are actually Prabhupāda's disciples. They may be present in the audience, and that may put some pressure on me to direct my thoughts in their direction, but I really prefer to speak to people who won't be challenging.

My physical body doesn't like challenge and confrontation. It gives me headaches. Some may thrive on this opposition, but I don't look forward to it. I prefer to talk about spiritual life with like-minded persons—to read about Kṛṣṇa's pastimes, especially with those who like to talk about Kṛṣṇa and Rādhā in Vraja.

Even as I write this I'm looking at a picture of Prabhupāda. We are always in his shelter, but we also feel always lacking, not inquiring deeply enough into the nature of the spiritual master and how to please him—not doing anything enough. There should be more.

March 15
Trinidad, West Indies

Dear friends,

I'm composing this letter around seven in the morning in Trinidad. I want to tell you some of the events of our last night's travel. I won't tell you about the Hindu Christian and his friend with whom we spoke before we got on the plane. I wrote about that in my diary. But that talk set the tone for the night because I felt so alert and excited afterwards. I felt that I had done all right in speaking with him. I had held my own. After all, I've been a devotee for so many years, I ought to have some sense of control and confidence when I speak to a couple of Christians, both of whom were younger than I.

So on the plane I was feeling wide awake and confident. I began to think that I could be more outgoing and giving to the devotees and others I meet. The stewardess asked if we wanted anything to drink. Madhu wanted mineral water, but they didn't have any. She said to him, "How about water-water?" No, he didn't want any. Then she turned to me and I said, "I'll take some water-water." The stewardess liked that. I was feeling lighthearted that I could relax in the world and talk with people as a devotee. We are always aware of being a disciple and a representative of Prabhupāda, but if we can keep that identity and be nice to people, even be lighthearted and show people that we're not uptight because we have Kṛṣṇa—then isn't that a kind of preaching too ?

Our plane landed in Trinidad and as we were disembarking, the young man who waves the flashlights to guide the plane came up to us. He was a dark young man of Indian descent, and he said he was a friend of my disciple Baladeva. He said Baladeva would be waiting for us inside after we got through with the luggage. This was an unusually friendly gesture, to have a member of the ground crew meet you. I thought at first he might be able to get us through immigration quickly, but it was just a greeting with information that we already knew.

At immigration Madhu went through first. When it was my turn, the Trinidadian immigration official said, "I have just told your colleague that since you don't have a preaching permit, you are not to preach at any type of gathering while you are here. You understand?" I replied, "Yes." I knew this was the little game that one always plays on entering Trinidad. To get the speakers permit takes weeks, so we usually don't get one. But I've never been given such a direct warning. It left me thinking, "Is this fellow going to attend one of our temple programs, hear me glorifying Lord Caitanya on Gaura-pūrṇimā, and then tell me I'm violating a national law?" I tried not to worry about it.

When we got into the luggage area, we waited as usual. A flashing sign with red letters passing from left to right said "Vat 19 Rum is the spirit of Trinidad." A young man, another employee of the airport, came up to us and said he was also Baladeva's friend. He came to help us with our luggage. For a moment I thought that he might be able to expedite our way through customs, but then I realized he, like the other fellow, could do little to help us through that line. After a long wait, the luggage came, and Madhu let him pick our suitcases off the revolving carousel and place them on the wheeled cart. Then we pushed them up to the green line. The official on the line was passing everyone through quite quickly. When he came to us he asked a few questions, looked in our luggage, and told us to go over to the red line where our luggage would be inspected. "Nothing personal," he added. I shook my head sadly to indicate I didn't approve. Although it was now midnight, we had to go through the wearying ritual of opening the luggage. The inspector, a big man of Hindu descent, remarked that Madhu packed the luggage very neatly, a compliment that we didn't savor under the circumstances. Then he asked "What's in this box? What's in this?" Telling him was not good enough; we had to open the boxes and show him everything. That went on for fifteen or twenty minutes.

When we finally pushed our luggage through, our young friend was able to render some special service. He took all of our suitcases on a big carriage and wheeled them out to the car where Rājarṣi and Baladeva were waiting. Then we went to Baladeva's house and slept for a few hours. Now it's morning and I'm chanting japa. I'm ready to go to the "South" temple.

Those are my little adventures. I didn't want the experience to pass without telling you, and I couldn't tell you later with the same vividness. I don't know if it constitutes a bonafide preaching letter, but I wanted to share it with my friends.

March 16
Trinidad

To those who "worship" life itself,

Sometimes when I talk with people like yourselves I feel a little intimidated because you claim that Kṛṣṇa consciousness doesn't give enough attention to life. In the Kṛṣṇa conscious philosophy, we teach that the material world is actually an illusion because it is temporary. The material manifestation is real in that it comes from God and is God's eternal energy, but it is unreal because it does not last. Reality lies in what is eternal. However, we don't dismiss this temporary manifestation. Human existence is certainly poignant and full of opportunity. This life is a brief time in which a person can develop surrender to Kṛṣṇa to the fullest extent. This assures his going to the eternal spiritual world in the next life. So the opportunity of this life is very precious.

I think my main point to you is this: your religion is contained within mine. By this I don't mean to deride or minimize your religion. Rather, I mean this as a prelude to a friendly exchange. We are part of the same family. But if one simply "worships" life without the transcendental goal, it is hardly a religion.

I have a particular viewpoint in Kṛṣṇa consciousness. As someone who tries to serve through writing, I have a proclivity to capture the experience of life as it passes. This is Kṛṣṇa's time and place; how can I reject it? And by writing down the day I can see how well I used this precious life. Kṛṣṇa says in the *Bhagavad-gītā:* "To one who always sees Me everywhere and sees everything in Me, He is never lost to Me and I am never lost to Him."

So I guess I'm also writing this letter indirectly to devotees of Kṛṣṇa—to remind them that attention to temporary phenomena is important if the temporary phenomena includes our very life in this body and our attempt to become Kṛṣṇa conscious. When we communicate with each other and share what is valuable, it's not just that we quote the *śāstra* to each other or talk about the times that existed in Vedic culture five hundred or five thousand years ago. We have to talk about the present and share our love according to time, place, and person.

I request you, worshippers of life itself, please don't accuse this devotee of not thinking as you think. It's something that's always there consciously or unconsciously, even when I perform the transcendental activities in our temple. We can't escape it—the sensory input, the temporary thought, the sense of time passing, and the impossibly rich texture of this temporary life. This is especially true for someone like me who is in a transitional stage: I have my two feet in this world and my eyes on the spiritual world.

I'm so grateful to Prabhupāda that I'm not a confused piece of flotsam going through this life and making vain gestures or laments about the mutability of all things. I see this world, in all its mutability, as Kṛṣṇa's energy. And sometimes I take a stronger attitude and see it as insignificant.

But I have my moments of appreciation and an enduring respect that everything is sustained by Kṛṣṇa, even in this material world.

Worshippers of life itself, I would like to hear from you, see any poems you write, or pictures you paint of this world. But my deepest hankering is for the spiritual world. Therefore my best use of this present time is to absorb myself in the transcendental material that brings me directly to Kṛṣṇa.

March 16
Trinidad

About a helpless creature,

In one of my visits downstairs to the adjoining toilet and shower rooms, I saw a large roach lying on its back, kicking its legs in the air. I call it a roach, but I think it was actually much bigger than a roach. When I saw him there, I first thought of setting him on his feet again. But I really didn't want to touch him. Anyway, sometimes you get involved in helping some creature and it doesn't work. Then I thought as I walked away that I might write him a letter. The best communication would be to chant in his ear: Hare Kṛṣṇa Hare Kṛṣṇa, Kṛṣṇa Kṛṣṇa Hare Hare/Hare Rāma Hare Rāma, Rāma Rāma Hare Hare.

We have to pass so many struggling creatures lying by the roadside without helping them. One day we too will be there and hope that some "good Samaritan" will stop for us. Although I failed to stop and chant to this creature, not only because of my slowness as a preacher, but also my lack of full faith in the holy name, I don't want to just drop the incident without writing a letter to remind myself to stop next time, and stoop and chant.

March 17
Trinidad

To the shoes of Abhaya dāsa,

There you are, sitting by the door. Nowadays they make even the smallest baby shoes look like track shoes. And yours, Abhaya, are "Amazing Spiderman" shoes with designs of spider webs on the front and back, and a picture of Spiderman himself. Of course, you can't even talk yet, so you don't know what's written on your shoes. But maybe when your father was buying them, he thought you would like Spiderman, or perhaps you even pointed them out and demanded them.

Prabhupāda says that when a father looks at his son's shoes, he feels love for his child. In the same way, one who is a lover of Kṛṣṇa sees Kṛṣṇa everywhere in the universe. He sees everything as the energy and extension of the beloved Supreme Personality of Godhead. We can do this to some degree, but those who are in the Vraja-*rasa* see Vṛndāvana everywhere. They see the Yamunā in every river and Govardhana in every hill—even in the rivers and hills of Trinidad. Of course, this vision cannot be imitated. It's a long, long way from the heart of this poor *sādhaka* to the ecstasy of seeing Kṛṣṇa and Vṛndāvana in the varied objects of this world. Therefore I write a letter to Abhaya's shoes. I think of his father who sees these shoes and is filled with love for his child. These "Amazing Spiderman" shoes: tiny, amazing, and white.

March 18
Trinidad

Dear friends,

I'm staying near the temple in a house owned by Kṛṣṇa-kṛpa dāsa, a disciple. Right now I'm looking out a window at palm trees and the cloudy sky. It's a sultry day in Trinidad. This house where I'm staying is in a lonely area; it's quiet, except on the weekend when people get drunk and play their radios. Right near the house is about an acre of land which devotees are cultivating. All this morning in the heat of the sun, one man with a freshly-shaven head and no hat has been working. He has been irrigating and digging, helped by a woman who is working as his partner. I wouldn't dream of working out there with a bare head. He's young and strong, but still it's hard for him.

I have been staying inside this house, but I have been working too. For an hour and a half I met with a devotee who has resigned from his job. He is now working full-time with devotees and facing the reality of that. He runs into difficulty because he makes demands. Our discussion was delicate. I tried to encourage him while at the same time hint how he might improve his relations with others. I have two more meetings scheduled today. I'm writing this in a brief interlude before lunch.

It's intensely distracting here. I even chanted less *japa* than usual this morning because of it. They are trying to draw me into squabbles and the managerial crises over the possible loss of their temple. I'm not a manager here, but just hearing about it is draining. Now I'm behind schedule in my chanting, behind in my writing, and my inner life is filled with distracting thoughts. I have to admire and pay obeisances to devotees who are willing to live with this all the time. Devotees who take on management are selfless workers; they are performing as heavy an austerity as someone who works all day in the hot sun. I offer my obeisances to them.

But I also have to defend my own service which demands neutrality and a calm center. Since I've been here, the verses in the morning *Bhāgavatam* classes have stressed that the most important thing is *śravaṇam-kīrtanam.* The real perfection of humanity is to hear and chant about the qualities and pastimes of Kṛṣṇa and His holy names. These verses are coming at a time when I myself am thinking that this is what I want to do. I have come to a place of intense dispute, but the *Bhāgavatam* tells us to rise above this and chant and hear. I try to follow that instruction.

I don't want to get drawn into management; nor do I want to be irresponsible. To some degree I can't be aloof from the problems that cause devotees to suffer; I have to give them counseling. This has made me introspective. I keep doing what I'm doing, but I'm aware that I too am part of this society. I work under the GBC and I want to satisfy them. I'm hoping to be accepted in the way I see myself contributing.

Before I close this letter, I want to tell you a funny story of something that happened in *Śrīmad-*

Bhāgavatam class. I was talking about what it takes to go back to Godhead. We were acknowledging that on the one hand, Bhaktisiddhānta Sarasvatī said we should finish up our business as soon as possible in one lifetime. But then we have to recognize that we have to be completely pure and have specific love for Kṛṣṇa before we can go back to Him. While I was emphatically making this point, I noticed a Hindu man standing like Hiraṇyakaśipu with both hands raised in the air. He was on one foot and his other foot was placed at an angle against his leg. He had a serious look on his face, so I glanced at him and continued, "We can't go back to Godhead by standing on one leg, but only by achieving love of Kṛṣṇa." I just kept going, but the devotees burst out laughing. When I looked over again, the man had sat down.

I guess that's all for now. Thank you for listening and for being who you are. I hope that I will also be able to listen to you and have the *prīti-lakṣaṇam** exchanges described in the *Nectar of Instruction*. If we're lucky, we will be able to get out of this entanglement and some day, talk purely of the more pleasurable topics of Kṛṣṇa's pastimes and qualities.

---

* The six symptoms of love shared by one devotee and another as described in the *Śrī Upadeśāmṛta* Text 4

March 19
Trinidad

Dear mosquitoes,

This is a warning: if you come near me, I'll kill you.

I realize this is about as silly as you can get, thinking you can write letters to mosquitoes. I might as well write a letter to the fireflies. I could say, "You look enchanting the way you light up spots of darkness in the tropical jungle of this backyard." I might as well write a letter to the little white cat. Its face has been roughed-up and it's not so pretty to look at. It roams around this house where they're letting me stay. It probably kills mice and rats. But this letter is a warning to the mosquitoes.

Life is rich and I'm trying to record it in a Kṛṣṇa conscious way. There's so much I want to say that I can't say it all. There are different people on my mind. I am thinking about Vṛndāvana, thinking about how to advance in Kṛṣṇa consciousness, thinking things I don't dare to say, things that are here and things that are far away. Out of all this richness, it's natural to think of somebody to share it with. If you're lucky you can find a person, a close friend, and pour out everything. But when you can't do that, then you can write a letter to a mosquito and tell him to bug off or you'll kill him.

The poor mosquitoes can't respond not only to my letter, but to my warning. All they know is blood. That's the way the material energy is constructed. That's their karma from the past. I suppose if I were an extremely renounced saint like the leper Vāsudeva, I wouldn't bother the mosquitoes in their attempt to suck my blood. And to some degree, I'm trying to tolerate them. Therefore, although I'm giving the mosquitoes this warning, I'm going to avoid their association entirely by getting under the mosquito net. This letter is just for any stray ones that I happen to encounter before I get under that net.

P.S. When I went in the backyard to dictate this letter to the mosquitoes, I looked out and saw the rich darkness just before night, the fireflies everywhere, and the white cat roaming around in the dark.

March 19
Trinidad

Dear builder of dreams,

This is interdepartmental mail. It doesn't require U.S. postage and yet I don't know where exactly to send it. Since there's always a person in charge, there must be someone who builds my dreams. So I'm writing to you, unconscious dream-building self.

Last night I had a dream about the artist's life. I was the lead character and I was doing some kind of graphic artwork. Then the scene changed and I was a literary artist and suffering because I had no means of livelihood. I was misunderstood, but remained dedicated, obscure, talented, and faithful.

There was nothing in the dream overtly Kṛṣṇa conscious. When I awoke I was sorry I didn't have the sense to chant Hare Kṛṣṇa. Then I thought to direct a letter to you, my dreaming self. Why can't you chant Hare Kṛṣṇa?

Since you are a hidden, unconscious self, I don't expect you to reply, but I want to make a sincere request for Kṛṣṇa conscious dreams. Perhaps you're not able to comply. Perhaps you need input from an even deeper level and, after all, you're just doing your job like anyone else. You produce dreams according to the sensory input you're given.

Dream-self, I think that you are a deep person. I don't know who else would need to give you input. We're all just fragmented voices speaking impurely because the pure spirit soul has not been uncovered. This is especially obvious in the dreams which are almost entirely devoid of direct Kṛṣṇa consciousness. Therefore, I am making this request. I understand you prefer subtle suggestions, so I won't order you.

I spend such a large amount of every twenty-four hours sleeping. It would be better if the dream episodes could be devotional, with sincere prayers, chanting, and service to Rādhā and Kṛṣṇa rendered with body, mind, and words. This is my suggestion: please give me Kṛṣṇa conscious dreams.

March 20
Trinidad

Dear Śrīla Prabhupāda,

Please accept my humble obeisances at your lotus feet. All glories to you.

I'm writing this sitting on the back porch of a house just outside the wall of the temple. In about fifteen minutes, I'll go to the packed *kīrtana* hall and deliver a Gaura-pūrṇimā lecture. I have one of my headaches and have had to lie down all day, but I wanted to write to you before I went inside.

I wrote in my diary today that I don't know Lord Caitanya or Rūpa Gosvāmī or Rādhā-Kṛṣṇa, but I do know you, Śrīla Prabhupāda. Of course, I don't actually know you—you are beyond me—but you know what I mean. You know me. There is a difference in my experience of you and my experience of the Lord and His associates.

By your grace, I'm beginning to know them also, but it's such a fight against *māyā*, Śrīla Prabhupāda. Cynicism and skepticism are always ready to creep back in unless we're watchful.

Prabhupāda, my mind is so uncontrolled. Devotees often ask me how to control the mind. I tell them what Kṛṣṇa says—just bring the uncontrolled mind under the control of the higher self. I do that, but it's embarrassing when we still think of *sādhu-nindā*. I don't know if I'll ever be free of it, but by your grace, Śrīla Prabhupāda, I'll be a fighter in your footsteps and will always bring the mind back under the control of my higher self.

Please save me from any sojourn, even for a moment, in *sādhu-nindā* and *guru-aparādha.*

Prabhupāda, by your grace I will be able to speak about Lord Caitanya today. I've chosen a song by Narottama dāsa Ṭhākura, and I'm going to read parts of your purport on it and comment on that. I'll feel safe with your *vāṇī.* You say that Lord Caitanya's movement is easy. You also say it's pleasing because it's just chanting and dancing and taking *prasādam.* The guests here in Trinidad will be in that mood. They're a simple crew, and they'll be sweaty and gathered together. This "dancing white elephant" of yours from North America will tell them this good news. They'll be happy to hear it. Just chant, dance, and take *prasādam.*

You also say that if we chant Lord Caitanya's names, we can gain love of God. And this love is permanent, not like the lust of the material world.

At the conclusion of your purport, you translate Narottama dāsa Ṭhākura's line that anyone who chants the name "Gaurāṅga" is a dear associate. So I'll emphasize that whatever position of life one is in, if they chant Hare Kṛṣṇa, crying out sincerely to the Lord, they become dear devotees of the Lord.

So I've got a nice Gaura-pūrṇimā lecture lined up by your grace. I have no *gaura-bhakti,* no *kṛṣṇa-bhakti* and no *śakti*—just a headache and the usual attachments and pettiness. But by your grace, I'm sure it will be an acceptable lecture. Then I'll come back and honor *prasādam* and try to take rest so that this pain goes away overnight.

I look forward to having good energy tomorrow to bring the mind under the control of my higher self. And to avoid offenses. Everything depends on you, Prabhupāda, and I'm fortunate that I can depend on such an unquestionably pure, strong devotee. You are the one who will carry me through. I just have to follow you. Let me grow, Prabhupāda, on my own, in my love for Rādhā and Kṛṣṇa, and let me take all relevant instructions from the six Gosvāmīs. But let me always do so as your menial servant.

Wherever you are today, Prabhupāda, please accept my humble obeisances and my desire to be able to think more clearly, deeply, and purely. I wish to be able to help others because I myself am connected to Kṛṣṇa and Rādhā. Then you will be proud of me. And then we can meet again and I can serve you in a liberated condition with no hang-ups. All glories to you, Prabhupāda, and your work in all the three worlds.

March 21
Trinidad

To two delicate mushrooms,

I think you are mushrooms. I just bent down to look at one of you, and by mistake, I broke one of your stems. You look like something that has grown up overnight, not like the mushrooms with the big parasol tops that we see in the north. Anyway, my thoughts go to you because you look like two good, silent persons with whom I can talk here in the backyard outside the wall of the Trinidad temple. I'm sorry that I broke one of your stems. Probably I have killed you, although your partner is still standing upright. In any case, I don't think you have a long life, so I'm asking you to just hear me for a little while.

We human beings are so presumptuous the way we use material nature. The Bible says that animals are under the dominion of man, but does that mean they should be killed by us? There are ways to use our superiority to benefit animal species and human-kind alike. Yet in another sense, the whole idea of superiority is presumptuous.

Lord Caitanya says that we should think ourselves lower than a blade of grass. All the blades of grass, or at least clumps of grass, are *jīvas*, spirit souls, and in their spiritual, atomic size, they are just as good as I am.

Therefore they can certainly be confidants if you wish to pour your heart out to them. I think I came here, dear mushrooms, to tell you about myself and about my tendency to feel guilty when I compare myself to my Godbrothers. That guilt is not deep; it's more a matter of self-defense. I want to protect my own service and who I am. I don't want to be caught up in another's service or be made to think I should do something other than what I am doing. I want to surrender in my present service, and that includes writing letters to mushrooms and to baby boy's shoes. It's important and I want to defend it. In order to do it nicely, I can't always be detracted by these guilt trips, and neither can I have my time taken up in somebody else's service. My service includes plenty of other people's services in terms of counseling and helping and hearing.

So my dear mushrooms, I came to you to speak this little self-defensive line. I wanted you to hear me. I guess I will go away feeling better and more satisfied. That's what often happens when we share our troubles with someone who receives them silently and pleasantly—we feel relieved. In such a relationship we don't really care so much about the other person, only that they be a receptacle. But it is definitely a service that living beings offer to people when they listen. You've been listening so nicely, and in exchange, I broke one of your stems. I am sorry for that.

At least by approaching you I have found greater appreciation for yourselves and all the humble living entities in the backyard who cannot move. (Here's a fellow who can move, a caterpillar roaming the hard earth with many feet. You are all living here while rapacious birds and other creatures roam around looking for you. They see you as food—*jīvo jīvasya jīvanam.)*

And this is also Kṛṣṇa consciousness, to squat down next to the earth and see all of you and chant Hare Kṛṣṇa. It is Kṛṣṇa consciousness to see things up close, not only to speak to unburden yourself to a mushroom, but to listen to the lowly creation. Kṛṣṇadāsa Kavirāja Gosvāmī writes that the trees and lowly plants take part in the *kīrtana* of the nonmoving living entities. It is more than a poetic metaphor. If we get close to the earth, we can hear their *kīrtana*.

We usually stride arrogantly and even violently through this material world, crushing everything around us with no consideration for anything. I especially should extend myself to lowly creatures because I'm often too shy to extend myself to human beings. People are so demanding! But the lower creatures are not. So let me try to put in a good word for you fellows. Let me try to remind other humans who read letters to be kind to the earth and to sometimes stop and listen to what the lesser creatures are saying. Of course, on the material level, the lesser creatures are as rapacious as the humans, but if we get really close to them, sometimes we can sense that we are all spirit souls, brothers and sisters. If nothing else, it helps to purify a human being. Isn't this also included in Lord Caitanya's teaching: "One should think oneself lower than a blade of grass, be more tolerant than a tree, devoid of all sense of false prestige, and offer all respects to others. In such a state of mind one can chant the holy name of the Lord constantly"?

I'm going to chant my sixteenth round in your vicinity now, dear mushrooms. Please listen.

March 22
West Coast Demerara, Guyana

Dear friends,

Let me just begin with some of the things I thought of this morning on my way to Guyana. I didn't go very deep. When you travel, it's hard to go deep because you have to keep your attention on the formalities of showing your ticket and your boarding pass and going through immigration and talking to the people who are interested only in these external things. Like this morning in the Trinidad airport lounge, large, prominently placed televisions loudly broadcast a cricket game. That was at 3 A.M., so how deep can you go when you're being bombarded by that at three in the morning? Somehow (probably because I'm not so interested in cricket), I was able to hear the holy names to some degree and go on with my chanting. And also because Trinidad is so third-world and has a Hindu background, I didn't feel intimidated about being a Hare Kṛṣṇa devotee. I wasn't afraid of somebody hearing my prayers. I did the same thing on the airplane—continued chanting. But as I said, I couldn't go very deep. I wrote a few things in my diary, thought about bodily maintenance, and tried to think of a topic on which to lecture when I got here.

When we arrived, things went predictably well. I should never take that for granted, but should thank Kṛṣṇa. Everything could go wrong and sometimes it does, but Kṛṣṇa protects us and allows us to perform our duties. Whether circumstances are good or bad, what's important is to do the right thing. For example, when we got through customs we met the devotees. It was only a short meeting and then we had to get in separate cars and drive off. I wanted to give them more somehow. They had all risen so early just to meet me, but what could I give them? Nothing, just a few words before getting into the car. So I spontaneously embraced each man. Do what you can, give what you can.

The drive to the temple was pleasant. It was 6 A.M. Guyana time and the sun wasn't up yet, but there were piles of thick clouds in an otherwise clear sky. Everything was gradually turning light. At first we could hardly see people on the road, but there were hitchhikers trying to stop our cars. I talked with Paramātmā dāsa, who was sitting in the back seat with me. I asked him, "Materially speaking, what is the country like now? Is it getting worse?"

He told me that for the last year Guyana has been improving in many ways. They now have a free market and they've given up their Marxist restrictive rule. Things are more open. As he spoke, I compared my present feelings with how I felt on my earlier visits to Guyana. I used to be so afraid. Perhaps it was a more fearful time under the dictatorship. I thought that I might be imprisoned or attacked. I was afraid, especially because I had heard so many stories about how the blacks were oppressed and aggressive. Partly I was exaggerating. It was all so strange, such a culture shock. This morning as we went past the houses, I felt this contrast.

The houses are built on stilts above the ground. Instead of glass panes, the windows have horizontal slats or shutters, and it creates a strange effect. I still remember the first time I came to Guyana. I arrived at night, and when I looked at the houses and saw those slats with the light coming through, I thought it looked eerie. This was around Jim Jones' time and the mass suicide of his cult in Guyana.

Anyway, I am still not completely relaxed here. But then where do I feel relaxed? America is also a scary place. In fact, I'm glad when I'm out of America. I feel like the long arm of the law will not reach me here in Guyana. Anything can happen in America. It seems a more likely place where I'm going to get "caught" and made to do something. So in that sense, I feel like I'm more on the loose here. There are advantages and disadvantages to each place. No place is home.

The best time is when I'm on a writing retreat. Then I do exactly what I want, on my own schedule. The free will expresses itself and I try to go deeply into my Kṛṣṇa conscious writing and self-examination. The only hitch is that it's temporary. I have my days marked on a calendar. One by one I cross them off until they're all gone. There is no place where I am relaxed or free. Every place has the same pinch.

The real point is to become Kṛṣṇa conscious in any situation. I felt that today. I felt it was possible to attain Vṛndāvana consciousness even in Guyana. The main thing is to hear about Kṛṣṇa.

Therefore, it was so nice to speak from the *Manaḥ-śikṣā* prayers in which Raghunātha dāsa Gosvāmī says to his mind: "Dear mind, please give up your pride, and with intense and extraordinary love, worship the spiritual master and Vṛndāvana and the people of Vṛndāvana and Rādhā-Kṛṣṇa." It's possible to do that even in Guyana.

March 24
West Coast Demerara

Dear Dhruva dāsa, Pāṇḍava dāsa, Vātsalya dāsa, and Rādhikā-devī dāsī,

Please accept Prabhupāda's blessings from me. All glories to Śrīla Prabhupāda. Your names appeared on a list I was given yesterday of disciples of mine who are "not active" in Guyana. In other words, you don't practice Kṛṣṇa consciousness anymore and that also means you don't consider me your spiritual guide.

I was speaking quite a bit yesterday to different groups of devotees, but I haven't been able to address you. I suppose, too, there's not much I want to say. I take a live-and-let-live attitude if somebody doesn't want to practice Kṛṣṇa consciousness. What am I supposed to do, beat you on the head? Anyway you won't make yourself available for any beating or any blessing or any instruction.

But I wouldn't mind hearing from you. I'm open to hearing any sad or angry tale you have to tell, perhaps about how other people disappointed you in the Kṛṣṇa consciousness movement. You're probably honest enough to admit that you aren't "into" the path of *bhakti* anymore. But you used to be. Whether it was an infatuation or a serious interest in Kṛṣṇa consciousness, I would like to appeal to you to reconsider taking up your practices.

Think now of what you're doing without Kṛṣṇa consciousness. Isn't it lacking? I mean, when you think about it deeply, doesn't your life lack a serious purpose that it used to have? Probably you haven't developed a philosophical skepticism, but have just become immersed in material duties and made excuses to yourself as to why that's all right.

You believe in God, don't you? Do you believe in Kṛṣṇa as the Supreme Personality of Godhead? Then why don't you turn to Him again?

Mainly I just want to drop you a reminder that you can file away in your heart. When fate turns, perhaps especially when you become unhappy, remember the promise of spiritual life and how you left it unfulfilled.

Anyway, don't forget us. Why not go to the New Pāṇīhaṭī temple sometimes and see Rādhā-Kṛṣṇa? You don't have to get involved in what you consider unpleasant exchanges with devotees there; just go for your own benefit, say hello to Kṛṣṇa, and take some *kṛṣṇa-prasādam.* And you can try to pray.

March 24
West Coast Demerara

To the devotee who fell asleep in the temple room,

It's embarrassing that I have to say this to you. I didn't notice at the time that you fell asleep during *japa;* someone told me about it afterwards.

It's embarrassing because just yesterday, you presented yourself as a guru, and, to make it worse, you gave a long lecture about inattentive chanting. Somebody even made a plea about how devotees get sleepy, but you were unrelenting. You said that if someone was so sleepy he or she should take rest; but when chanting we should be at our peak and give it our best time. You said these things and now today you fell asleep in our midst during the *japa* hour. You would be holding a bead between your fingers but no sound would come out. I noticed that when you got up and walked, you were all right, but as soon as you sat down, it happened again.

My advice is that you had better not stay in the temple room during *japa* if you're going to be dozing off.

Anyway, it serves you right if they take a good look at you and think, "This guy is a hypocrite. This guy is just like us, or worse." And isn't it true? You're older than they are and still you don't practice what you preach. Maybe you have some kind of deeper attachment to the practices. You're not going to quit. But I'm afraid you're not going to quit sleeping during *japa* either. I'm afraid you're going to go to your death dozing off.

Why not do yourself a favor and go up and take a nap?

March 25
West Coast Demerara

Dear person who will never visit the Uitvlugt center,

I'm writing this letter in the last moments of my candle's life. It has burned down in two days to its very bottom. It's flickering in front of a picture of the six Gosvāmīs and the other pictures I have on my altar in my room. This is not a romantic luxury; there is no electricity. In a few minutes I'll have to go down to *maṅgala-ārati,* which will probably be held by kerosene lamp.

I think the main purpose in writing this letter is that I want to describe the temple room. There's a unique flavor to it that somehow seems worth describing to you who will never come here.

The devotees have very little money in Guyana. The only reason they have a house like this is that one of the senior devotees, Bhūtādi Prabhu, was given it by his father. It's a big, three-story house. The temple room is quite large and it seems like two rooms without a divider. It has high ceilings and everything is made of wood—the floor, the ceiling, the walls. Everything is stained the same dark lacquer. This makes the room dark no matter what time of day it is. Even in bright sunlight the corners of the room are dark. There is only one fluorescent light high on the ceiling; even when there is electricity, the whole room is still cast in shadows. To me, being in that dark room will always embody the Guyanese experience, especially at *maṅgala-ārati.*

The devotees are lucky to have had this place now for about ten years. As with other ISKCON buildings, it's been the scene of continual devotional service. One of the outstanding features of this temple room is that as soon as somebody starts to dance, the whole building shakes. Even a passing car makes the building shake. You tend to think the whole house could shake apart, but somehow, just like the fragile devotional service of the devotees themselves—fragile because they're always prone to listen to their minds and fall into *māyā*—this house is somehow holding together. It is only Kṛṣṇa's grace. On a Sunday when the many guests start dancing, you just pray to Kṛṣṇa that the floor doesn't fall through then and there. Last Sunday we had just started to dance when the *pūjārī* stopped us because Nitāi-Caitanya-candra were shaking.

There are many other things I could say, but I'm in the last moments of the candle light and also the last moments before *maṅgala-ārati.*

March 26
New Pāṇīhaṭī, Berbice, Guyana

My dear mind,

Recently I have been reading *Manaḥ-śikṣā* to the devotees. Raghunātha dāsa Gosvāmī asks his mind to develop intense, extraordinary love for the spiritual master, the land of Vṛndāvana, the *vraja-vāsīs,* the Hare Kṛṣṇa mantra, and Rādhā and Kṛṣṇa. And he asks his mind to give up pride. We have been discussing how we can actually apply these exalted teachings to our own lives.

The mind is always pestering, always diverting us from the goal of spiritual life. Arjuna was right when he said that to control the mind is like trying to control the wind.

My dear mind, I would like to reason with you and ask you to be a better friend in Kṛṣṇa consciousness. Please don't take offense if I point out some of your qualities that make life with you difficult. One thing is, you are always experiencing so much distaste. I know you feel you are faithfully reporting what the senses have discovered, but you know you're supposed to control the senses. When you constantly register all this distaste, it's very uncomfortable. In a word, you are fastidious. Things have to be exactly right and even then you're not satisfied. Why do you register all this dissatisfaction? It's especially problematic when the senses range around the room or over the devotees and start to find fault: this one has an odd-shaped body, this one is not very intelligent, this one is too proud. These are all subtle forms of Vaiṣṇava *aparādha.*

My dear mind, you may say, "Well what am I supposed to do, cease to exist?" No, I believe in the Vedic statements that the mind is part of the subtle body and will always continue to live, so I cannot snuff you out. Nor do I want to. But you're supposed to be a spiritual person and not so attached to the material body or to the likes and dislikes you're always reminding me about. Why can't you be more subdued? Then we would actually come closer to liberation from this constant mental life.

My dear mind, you should go to the Hare Kṛṣṇa mantra even if in the beginning it means all you can do is pay attention to the timing of each round and to the sound of your voice. Stay simple.

And prepare to be disciplined. Ready or not, my duty is to take you from wherever you wander and bring you back under the control of my higher self. Don't resist me; let me take hold of you for the good of both of us, because without your cooperation, I cannot become Kṛṣṇa conscious. Kṛṣṇa consciousness means the mind is fixed on Kṛṣṇa; *man-manā bhava mad-bhakto,* "Think of Me," Kṛṣṇa says. Let's pray that Kṛṣṇa will make you a better mind for me and that you won't always be running back to the past, worrying about the present, dwelling on the body, or diving into the muck. You'll be serviceable.

I think that it's important that I ask your cooperation. I promise that there are better things and better times ahead if we apply ourselves. And you should know that I'm not going to let you get away with roaming all over the universe. I'm going to do as the poet Govinda dāsa suggests: I'm going to worship the lotus feet of Rādhā and Kṛṣṇa with my mind.

March 28
Paramātmā's house
Guyana

My dear friends,

I'm dictating this letter in a house where I don't have much privacy, so I'm speaking in a low voice. The walls don't reach the ceiling; someone in the next room could easily overhear me if I speak too loudly.

Why is it that I want privacy? What is this letter anyway? After I compose the letter I'm willing to have people see it, but now it's "oh, so private."

My dear Lord Kṛṣṇa, please have mercy on this sinner. My dear Śrīmatī Rādhārāṇī, please engage me in Your service.

Sometimes Kṛṣṇa writes letters to Rādhā or to the other *gopīs*, and sometimes the *gopīs* write letters and pass them to Kṛṣṇa. I'm not able to take part in such letter exchanges, but I'm thinking about them. I'm also thinking, "What good are these letters in which I tell my close friends what happened to me in my plane travels?" They're willing to hear and I'm glad for that, but why don't I tell them about Rādhā and Kṛṣṇa? Or better yet, why aren't I writing to Rādhā and Kṛṣṇa Themselves? Why don't I write letters to Rādhā's *sakhīs?* I'm not yet qualified. So I have to write to the devotees whom I know in this world. And to be honest, I have to tell them the things that mean a lot to me. That sometimes means telling about my bodily condition and things that happen as I travel.

But everyone should know—or I should know—that I really want to speak to the *vrajavāsīs*. Let's say I wish that I wished I could write to them. Is that clear? I don't wish for it now. I wish that my heart's essence would actually be a desire to be involved in Kṛṣṇa's pastimes with *vrajavāsīs*, and thus I would be thinking of those exchanges.

Maybe I'd be thinking of a letter that Rādhārāṇī wanted to write and which I could carry for Her. I probably wouldn't do much letter-writing of my own. Maybe I'd write to a *sakhī* and tell her some of Rādhā-Kṛṣṇa's pastimes. Maybe I would write to some flower merchant—if there is such a thing in the spiritual world—to make sure that the best flowers are picked so I could make a nice garland for the Divine Couple All my affairs would be bound up in those pastimes. Letter-writing would not be about how I got out of Guyana or how I went to Europe.

I'm writing this letter to let you know that this is my desire. Maybe in the future you will receive a letter from me in that spirit when you and I have our *siddha-svarūpa*. We should look forward to that even now, and impel our minds in the right direction by hearing *kṛṣṇa-kathā* from the right source. You see now why I'm speaking very softly and don't want to be heard in the next room—because this is confidential.

As for why I write about material details, it's hard to say. I think it has to do with survival, with a prayer to be protected, with my heartbeat, with fear, with desire for intimacy. These things are dear to a conditioned soul. He knows that he's in a particular place, and within that place he senses his existence. Therefore, when he sees things like a row of ants going up and down the wall in two-way traffic, or when he looks at the worn floor boards and the light coming through in gaps between them, or for that matter wherever he turns, whatever he feels, it has to do with existence itself. We cannot see the spiritual world directly through this material covering; but this is our existence in this material body and it is dear to us. Śrīla Prabhupāda says the reason we sense the preciousness of a moment is the material objects seem to scream, "This is existence!" is because we are spirit soul. Because we are embodied, we relate to other creatures and to the so-called dead material objects around us. That's why things are so dear to us.

Why then is the self *(ātmā)* dear to us? According to scripture, the individual soul is connected to the Supreme. Without connection to the Supreme, the soul cannot stand on its own. We need the Supersoul. So our love for self is actually connected to the Supreme Self. Although we cannot feel it now, we have a great reservoir of love which we want to give to the Supreme Self.

Actually, we're afraid. We're trying to cling to life, but it's temporary. Our lives are threatened at every moment. There's no happiness in material objects and we know it. We're trying to pray to Kṛṣṇa through the material surroundings. Those who haven't received Kṛṣṇa conscious knowledge sometimes sense a mystic presence, an awareness of the aliveness of all objects—but that's as far as they get. Devotees know what's beyond the wall of matter, but even we cannot see Kṛṣṇa face to face if our realization is only theoretical. We're stuck in this world looking at floorboards and ants and feeling breezes and thinking that somehow we cannot deny that this is important to us, because we feel it, because we're in this body.

This is why I want to write a letter to my friends and say that I'm here in a humble little house in Guyana. The wind is blowing through the open window. These are just mundane facts, but you, my friends may get a glimpse of what I'm trying to say. I have faith that Kṛṣṇa is behind everything and that the goal of life is to be with Kṛṣṇa, Rādhā, and the *sakhīs,* and to write letters back and forth in Their *līlā* instead of this kind of fearful letter-writing. For now, this is my truth. My friends will pick this up and know what I really mean to say. But that takes quite a friend, doesn't it? Such friends have to see through my words to my heart.

I am grateful to my close friends.

P.S. Paramātmā dāsa says he bought this house for the U.S. equivalent of $2.50. Now he's paid off the house and he has no bills to speak of. Right now in the front yard, cows are grazing with the calves. A tan calf sucks milk from a tan cow, who's standing patiently. These aren't Paramātmā's cows; they belong to a neighbor. But in the live and let live spirit, Paramātmā doesn't mind the cows wandering over to "his" front yard, eating the grass, and dropping their cow dung. Paramātmā is not one of those Guyanese men who dreams of going to the U.S. He visited the

U.S. a few years ago and after two weeks wanted to go back to Guyana. I can see why he likes to stay here. It's so simple here. If you're willing to accept it and not crave material amenities, you can do away with a host of material concerns—no expenses, no telephone, no lawn mower.

I advised Paramātmā to take advantage of his little home site and to try to peacefully read Prabhupāda's books everyday. He's already doing that, along with his preaching.

These things are also important for me to tell you; they're part of the whole letter I wrote above. As you know, the cows and calves are intimately connected with *kṛṣṇa-līlā,* so even seeing cows down here helps you remember Kṛṣṇa and Vṛndāvana.

April 1
Rome, Italy

Dear friends,

We have traveled by airplane for two days and two nights, moving from the Caribbean to England and now to Italy. I thought that I wouldn't be able to get up for *maṅgala-ārati* after all that travel because of a headache, exhaustion, and jet-lag, but fortunately we got here in time to take a night's rest and I made it to the temple in the morning. It's cold in Rome, especially after the tropics, and the faces of the people are so different from what I became accustomed to seeing in the Caribbean. The people here are bigger; their faces are fuller. Anyway, I had this thought. It's a material thought perhaps, but in a sense, it's an appreciation of Kṛṣṇa consciousness, especially of the International Society for Krishna Consciousness that Prabhupāda created.

It is wonderful that cultures all over the world practice Kṛṣṇa consciousness. Even holy persons in India cannot appreciate what Prabhupāda has done, because unconsciously, they may think that only Hindus who are trained from birth in pious families can practice Kṛṣṇa consciousness. But the fact is, the world is full of many cultures, of millions and billions of people. Kṛṣṇa wants them all to go back to Godhead. How can that happen?

It's happening by Prabhupāda's grace. I sense it when I go from the ISKCON temples of Guyana with their African-Hindu congregations to the

Italian temples filled with Mediterranean and European faces. Neither of these countries had a strong Vaiṣṇava culture, but they do now.

Indian-born *brāhmaṇas* may criticize the devotees for not doing certain things correctly, but how wonderful it is that the devotees are so sincerely chanting Hare Kṛṣṇa. And if they have their own ways of doing things in their temples, that's nice too. That's what gives ISKCON its particular flavor. When you go into the temple, you see not only the Vaiṣṇava spiritual culture, but the local culture as well, and there's something thrilling about that combination.

I also thought how fulfilling all this is for me. How could I ever have expected to be chanting in some exotic Roman commune with Italian men and women? As I paced back and forth and looked around, I saw the long-haired guests in their street clothes. They, more than the devotees, looked like the local people. It was exciting, exotic, something I could not have achieved without coming to Kṛṣṇa consciousness: the ability to travel widely and to enter into a kind of underground culture within any country.

Each country has so many underground cultures—the drug culture, the jazz culture, the writers', the artists'—how could a visitor ever enter them? But here I have entered into this spiritual underground—their address was published—in the cold predawn. I'm part of this inside group, the Hare Kṛṣṇa movement in Rome. We're chanting Hare Kṛṣṇa together and we know what it is. I feel gratitude and humility. I'm happy to be here and to serve them by speaking *Bhāgavatam*.

April 6
Mahāvākya dāsa's house,
Marche, Italy

Dear yellow flowers,

I'm picking you from the bush. You're easy to rip off because your stems are so soft. Now the big question is, why am I killing you? I'm not even sure that I am killing you, since after all, I'm only picking you off at the stems and the bush is still growing. It's difficult to figure out about spirit souls. If you pick an apple, you're not killing the apple because the spirit soul is in the tree itself; the apple is a by-product. But even if you consider a flower on a

bush as an entity, then I'm sacrificing these flowers to the pictures on my altar. I want to glorify Kṛṣṇa. But that makes me doubtful too. Am I actually offering the flowers, or am I just trying to create a nice atmosphere in my room for my own benefit? Are the pictures themselves to cheer me up and help me to be what I consider Kṛṣṇa conscious? These doubts make me unsure enough to stop picking flowers. Okay, I've got enough. Let's not pick so many. We pick flowers and put them in a glass of water, and after a few days, they die. I reason that if I didn't pick these particular flowers, they would die anyway. But still, we should be careful not to plunder our environment unnecessarily.

Dear yellow flowers, I'll try to find out your Italian name (and maybe your English name) so I can address this letter properly. What I wanted to say is, you're very pretty and you probably have some cousins who participate in Rādhā-Kṛṣṇa's Vṛndāvana pastimes.

Do you know that in Vṛndāvana, Vṛndā-devī decorates the forest for Kṛṣṇa's pastimes? Her work very much depends on flowers. In Vṛndāvana, there are flower garlands, flower earrings, flower crowns, even beds made of flowers. So you're a very important part of *kṛṣṇa-līlā*. There the spirit souls don't die; they're eternal. Exactly how it all works I don't know. But in this world, the *ācāryas* have encouraged us to pick flowers and use them in Kṛṣṇa's service. Therefore in all the temples in India, the Deities are offered many flower garlands. Flowers are also picked and sewn into garlands for saintly persons.

Everything has to be done thoughtfully. If you pick flowers, you can say they're for Kṛṣṇa, but you have to actually offer them, and without unnecessarily devastating a whole bush or wasting any or making the offering improper somehow.

April 7
Marche, Italy

Dear dawn chirping birds,

My boots are making so much noise on the gravel road that I can hardly hear you singing. Now I've stopped to listen. There are so many of you little fellows out there in the gray dawn that I can't tell one from the other. Please excuse me for not knowing your names or being able to distinguish your songs. I just want to say in this letter that life on earth is made pleasant by the songs of birds. And birds come from Kṛṣṇa. We hear the birds in Vṛndāvana, and even in the cities. They start to sing just near the end of our most intense, early morning *bhajana*.

Of course, I can't talk poetically about bird-song without eventually thinking how birds are spirit souls locked in little feathery bodies (which isn't so nice for them). The birds are also preying upon other creatures and eating them. But still, we cannot deny that the singing of birds enhances our humanness. It places us deep within our humble earthiness. Your songs bring us back to our childhoods. We remember all kinds of times, some of them hard times, when we were up in the morning and you were singing in the background.

You have hard times too, especially in winter when food is not so available. But you're always so faithful and dutiful and, at least to us, you sound joyful early in the morning.

I hope I don't ever get so old or self-absorbed that I stop noticing the spring and the birds' songs. I want to always be grateful that Kṛṣṇa is giving me another springtime on this earth. I think of it not in terms of mortal longevity, which is a vain pursuit, but in terms of my limited devotional service in this lifetime. I want to keep performing small acts of devotional service. I want to preach for another springtime, another summer. We belong to the earth, at least while we're here, and then we go away. It's Kṛṣṇa's place and His trademark is the singing of the birds.

Our appreciation of your music is part of our longing for the spiritual world. There will be birds there too. Early in the morning it's the birds' singing, impelled by Vṛndā-devī, that wakes Rādhā and Kṛṣṇa. Will the day come when I will be able to hear the birds like that, as warnings to Rādhā and Kṛṣṇa to wake up and go home? Will I ever have my own services to do as a servant of Their servants?

Let me share these thoughts with you, morning singers, here in Italy. In your ever-fresh quality and your undaunted courage, you are like gurus to me. I can take instruction and example even from your life of small consciousness. Hail to you, blithe spirits. Birds you never were.

April 11
Potenza Pizena, Italy

Dear friends,

The dawn sky is changing. It's so majestic and beautiful that it reminds me of Kṛṣṇa and Prabhupāda. There are big patches of agricultural land, some green, some brown, spread across gentle hills and valleys. The hills slope one into another. It's very pleasant-looking land, undulating under the sky in the early springtime.

It's a treat when I find quiet places to walk or sit and write to friends. For example, when we went to Jagannātha Purī, I couldn't talk on my walks because no matter how early I got up and went to the beach, there would always be people walking. I had a tape recorder with me and it was difficult to walk and speak privately without being interrupted.

In Puerto Rico, although the countryside is inviting, it is impossible to take walks because everyone has dogs. Big dogs run at you and bark no matter how early you get up. It makes walks impossible.

Ireland is a good place for walking. The Irish people don't seem to get up early, and either they have no dogs, or their dogs also sleep late. I appreciate this aspect of Irish culture, that the residents stay inside in the morning and let people like me walk around and talk and pray aloud and be happy. I've had some good luck in Irish places and hope to continue going there.

It's hard for me to find the time to take walks, and when I do find the time, there has to be a good place. I have a bad ankle, which also limits my walking. The morning walk is precious in that sense—I can walk for only an hour a day. I can't do any Vraja-*maṇḍala-parikramas* or *pada-yātrās*. This is my own private, daily *pada-yātrā*.

These walks are blissful, but it's only because I've had contact with Vṛndāvana and the devotees who reside there that I'm able to make my walks spiritual. Otherwise, it would be as though I were walking off a cliff, like a loony, talking to myself. Vṛndāvana is a different world. There are features of walks there that are greater than the attractions of walking anywhere else—to actually walk where Kṛṣṇa walked, or to walk where Raghunātha dāsa Gosvāmī walked. But I haven't found solitude in Vṛndāvana. It's a challenge: to find a place to walk, in solitude, in India, in the *dhāma*.

Here I am in Italy. I will describe for you what it's like. The houses are set quite far apart from each other, but there are dogs and they've been challenging me. Now it's getting worse because they're aware of the strange person who gets up early to walk. The dogs that belong to the nearest neighbors stop me even when I'm far away. How they detect me I don't know, but all three of them come running across the field, barking a warning to their owner. One of them wags his tail, so obviously he thinks this is fun. I walk in another direction and that sets off another dog. There are three different paths that I can take from the house, but one after another has been cut off. I almost know how far I can walk down a particular road before a dog starts barking. Then a light goes on inside the house and I turn around and go the other way until another dog starts barking. The barking makes me feel like a Frankenstein monster stalking around in my Wellington boots. I start to feel guilty and want to go back to the house and be a normal person. These dogs are not my friends.

The dogs will bark; the caravan will pass.

June 9
Finale Liguri, Italy

To preaching friends,

Padma Purāṇa was telling me about his preaching here in Finale Liguri. He and his wife (and now their one-year-old child, Nimāi) live in a little house. They have invited people from the area into their home over the years, and introduced them to Kṛṣṇa consciousness. Most of their guests are quite materially respectable—doctors, military officers, scientists, architects. These people have money, clean houses, culture, friends. It's not that they want to come to Kṛṣṇa consciousness because they don't have a good meal or need a place to sleep. In fact, they don't want to appear strange in the world in which they now live.

Padma Purāṇa told me in a good-humored way how one of his friends confidentially told him, "We very much like what you're doing and we want to help you, but we live in different worlds. I hope you respect our differences." Sometimes they indicate to him that they can't go any further. He has to honor this, be patient, keep setting his jolly, attractive example, and engage them in service in other ways. Eventually they come to him and ask for more.

Gradually Padma Purāṇa has been attracting them by his way of life, by his charm, and mainly by the convincing preaching he does from time to time. He and his wife have even taken one couple with them to India, and now another couple wants to go. They are going to build a temple here. So this is certainly preaching. It's very important to the Kṛṣṇa consciousness movement.

Padma Purāṇa told me he is inclined to this kind of preaching. That's why he has come here. He's no longer inclined to temple life; therefore he's able to attract people who don't want to live in a temple. He's enthusiastic about the particular angle he's presenting. His contribution is important, demonstrating that doctors, scientists, military officers, and other professional people can practice Kṛṣṇa consciousness and have devotees as friends.

Because I see Padma Purāṇa is excited about his service, it immediately strikes a chord within me that I should do what will make me enthusiastic. I should also work to spread Kṛṣṇa consciousness in whatever way I can. I think this is how we can happily hear each other and celebrate the many contributions that devotees are making. If I'm so convincing in my particular enthusiasm that people want to do the same service I'm doing, then that's fine. But let me always be aware when I'm speaking that there are people who can't do exactly what I am doing and I shouldn't hurt them by implying that their service is inferior. Only Kṛṣṇa is in a position to say whose service pleases Him the most. On an absolute platform, everyone is trying to please Kṛṣṇa, but this does not mean that Prabhupāda and Kṛṣṇa can only be pleased in one way.

No follower of Prabhupāda can avoid the conclusion that preaching is necessary. Some kind of positive response has to be made to Prabhupāda's preaching message. However, the particular application of preaching can be quite personal, depending on our capacity and nature. Successful preaching to devotees enthuses as many as possible to serve Kṛṣṇa; that is Prabhupāda's preaching spirit. When we're successful, we will make each devotee think to himself, not out of fear, but love, "How can I pick up this spirit?"

June 10
Finale Liguri

To those who give the greatest good,

Recently I have been thinking of what it means to be a preacher, to have preaching as one's vocation. This morning I read in *Caitanya-caritāmṛta* of Lord Caitanya's loving dealings with His devotees. Lord Caitanya was saying farewell, after four months, to the Bengali devotees who were returning home. Verse after verse, there is no purport. Then one verse states that Lord Caitanya said to Advaita Ācārya, "You please preach in Bengal and give Kṛṣṇa consciousness to everyone, even to the *caṇḍālas.*" Prabhupāda writes a long purport describing how Kṛṣṇa consciousness should be widely distributed. By example and by precept, the devotee is instructed that to give Kṛṣṇa is to give the greatest good.

There are so many people advertising themselves and their causes who are convinced that there is good in their message. There are also people who will say, "Yes, I've received this message and it's good." The Kṛṣṇa conscious preacher admits that there is partial good in the various messages, but the ultimate good must be permanent and must put us in our constitutional position—that of eternal servants of Kṛṣṇa. We're like the hand that derives its well-being and pleasure by serving the body's needs. The perfection of this service is found in Kṛṣṇa's dearmost devotees in Vraja. Those devotees are fully individual, self-willed, and fully liberated, yet they are utterly devoted to pleasing Kṛṣṇa in His pastimes. Kṛṣṇa's mother, Kṛṣṇa's friends, Kṛṣṇa's *gopīs*—each pleases Kṛṣṇa in a different way in a variety of *rasas*. They are the emblem of perfection.

Any cause that does not bring people to the Supreme is ultimately a dead end. The partial good of physical health, of mental well-being, of political improvement, of artistic culture—these things are undone by time. What to speak of causes that are foolish from beginning to end.

The devotee of Kṛṣṇa is not the most influential person in the world in terms of popular response. His books are not on the best-seller list. His speeches are not broadcast on television and relayed by satellite to millions of people all over the world. He's lucky if he can get fifty people a night to hear him. And as far as the wealthy and the powerful of the world, they regard Kṛṣṇa consciousness as insignificant. Yet a devotee is not deterred by this because he understands that this world is just a tiny outpost in the universe. In the absolute sense, the devotee is important and influential, whereas the kingpins of this world are like fireflies that shine for a short time and go out.

The devotee goes on helping even the few people who come to him. The preacher tells whoever comes forward about Kṛṣṇa; he helps them become Kṛṣṇa conscious. A preacher tends to want to help others even when he has needs of his own. And by doing that, Kṛṣṇa takes care of him. The person who talks about Kṛṣṇa finds he has no troubles, even if he is sick or without money. *Kṛṣṇa-kathā* cleanses the person who speaks, the person who hears, and even the place. To give Kṛṣṇa, the source of all benediction, is the ultimate charity.

June 10
Finale Liguri

To the family of Prabhupāda's followers,

This morning I was thinking again about the preaching vocation and how its "job security" is unlike that found in other kinds of work. I was imagining that I had to present identification papers during my travels. Someone was asking me for some proof of employment. I was explaining that for the past twenty-six years, I've been working for this spiritual movement and we don't have such papers. I don't receive pay.

I began thinking that it is sometimes a disappointment for devotees when they leave their work in the religious institution and go back to the secular job force and have nothing to show for their years of service. There have been no payments as such, and the material world categorizes their experience in the religious movement as mere proselytizing.

Yesterday, one devotee told me that some teenagers raised in the movement feel betrayed in two ways. First, they were promised from their earliest years that the Kṛṣṇa conscious society was wonderful, but it turned out, from their point of view, not to be so wonderful. Second, they were told that the material world was a bad place, but they're finding out that that's not true either. When I heard this I had to smile at the naiveté of these teenagers to think that we have been misrepresenting the material world and that actually, it is a happy place. Then I wondered why I don't feel betrayed even though I too see the many faults and disappointments in our institution.

Another devotee asked, "Are we supposed to be blind to the faults and just accept them?" "No," I said, "but despite the faults of the institution, we're not going to stop serving our guru or his mission. And we're not going to stop associating with devotees. Our spiritual master has saved us. We have already experienced the suffering of living in the material world. We tried to enjoy, but couldn't be happy. We began to see that this wasn't because we were misfits, but rather, because it is the nature of the material world. We gained wisdom from our experience and then happily took to Kṛṣṇa consciousness as the alternative."

Because my spiritual master saved me, I'm indebted to him, and I am tasting something sublime. Therefore, I won't leave and I won't become overwhelmed by examples of hypocrisy or corruption. I appreciate that the young people, in their honesty, become disillusioned when they see the gap between the idealistic descriptions of the Kṛṣṇa consciousness movement and what is actually practiced, but they are deluded if they think they can be happy as rock musicians or office workers. They'll have to learn for themselves, as we did. Yet it is the failure of the first generation of devotees that the movement is not such a wonderful place.

I began this train of thought while thinking of the preacher's vocation and his satisfaction with it. But preaching means many, many things. It means facing issues such as why the young people who grow up in the movement leave. Isn't that a preaching consideration? Or does preaching mean that we just go on giving lectures and distributing books and making up some explanation as to why those who live with us after a while decide not to live with us anymore? Preaching, Prabhupāda said, means to increase the family members. So a family has to stay together or the preaching is not effective.

The questions of encouraging the family members and sustaining the movement are not considered part of the classic description of preaching. Yet they are vital elements. No one person can be said to be involved in all aspects of preaching. There will be those who take responsibility for educating the children born in Kṛṣṇa consciousness and those who wander from place to place giving lectures and distributing books. Some with a greater capacity for management will become involved in many preaching activities. Like *kṣatriyas,* they will see that the *brāhmaṇas* are acting like *brāhmaṇas,* that the *vaiśyas* are acting like *vaiśyas,* and so on. But then managers may not have much time for meditation and *bhajana.* A responsible person will be aware that there are many issues to be decided and conditions to be improved and he will begin to work compassionately to improve his field of activity. At least his own area will be clean and attended to.

June 11
On the Road, France

Dear friends,

I was in the front of the cab, writing something in my diary. I would like to share it with you. I was saying that there are things in me that I want to express, but I can't. Or rather, my mind is so tired due to constant travel that I am unable to write or read *śāstra*. Instead, I've been remembering my high school days. By observing my trivial thoughts, I realized that I have a deeper level that is not accessible to me. And that's the main point—the goal of Kṛṣṇa consciousness is not accessible to me.

I intend to love Kṛṣṇa, but there is nothing much I can say about that because it's not very developed. Every living being is a pure soul and possesses the seed of a loving relationship with Kṛṣṇa, but our natures are covered over in different ways. Prabhupāda often said Kṛṣṇa consciousness means uncovering, cleansing, learning who we really are.

Some writers have a craving to express as much of the physical world and their impressions of it as possible, but ultimately it's not just facts that they want to convey. They want to remember experiences, but they want to infuse their remembrances with meaning. Writers may also feel that there is no meaning to be found in this world and they may want to decry every human's incoherency. As Thomas Wolfe said, "O lost, and by wind grieved, ghost come back again." Writers want to make music. They want to express inexpressible things. It's almost a desire to be God. I don't know what it is. I can't speak for them.

As for myself, it's not that I want to erupt and pour out all the things I've seen and done. These old memories are not so important. I don't usually find other people's reminiscences so interesting, so why should I think my reminiscences are interesting? They're only interesting to me because I have some love (attachment) for myself in this material body. That in turn makes me attached to the things I've done and seen. I've honored those experiences. So what?

And so we speed along, looking out at hills and highway and city congestion and commerce. Sometimes I shut my eyes because it's too much and it has no purpose. And then the mind, almost as if stimulated by the spinning wheels of our van, spins out so many scenes. I feel helpless in this shallow consciousness. When I try to chant Hare Kṛṣṇa, I don't have access to the holy name in worship, but I think, "Anyway at least I can say 'Hare Kṛṣṇa Hare Kṛṣṇa, Kṛṣṇa Kṛṣṇa Hare Hare/ Hare Rāma Hare Rāma, Rāma Rāma Hare Hare.' It's better than nothing."

Even my desire to communicate to you what I'm doing meets with the same dilemma. Namely, do I really have anything to say? But the basic facts are nice: we are traveling toward a Hare Kṛṣṇa temple where there are beautiful Rādhā-Govinda-Mādhava Deities. Our little van itself is a moving temple with pictures of Śrīla Prabhupāda, Pañca-tattva, and special portraits of Raghunātha dāsa Gosvāmī, Rūpa Gosvāmī, and finally, Rādhā and Kṛṣṇa.

Sometimes we just have to move ourselves from place to place like parcels, getting rudely bounced, and simply tolerating it. The white highway line shoots out the back of the van. The wind roars in the overhead vent. Madhu drives relentlessly, passing and stopping, passing and stopping. And I bounce around.

I am thinking of you and communing with you somehow or other. Let's just serve Śrīla Prabhupāda, although we know so little. Let's pray for faith, although we may not have much. Let's honor the other devotees and try to encourage each other to bring out the best in each of us, and to squelch those impulsive desires for sense gratification and sinful life. Everything is available in Kṛṣṇa consciousness; we don't have to fall down and suffer in the name of trying to be happy. Let's do our duty and endure the tedious times, knowing that within this self is a pure self. And one of these days, we will be able to come closer to reaching our goal of loving service to Kṛṣṇa.

June 14
New Māyāpura
France

Dear friends,

The first part of the morning program has ended and I have come out for a walk in the woods. I want to take you on a guided tour. What is a letter if not a desire for friends to be with you as you write? We may share news, but isn't the experience of time and place the message we most want to convey?

I am so glad to get out by myself. To get into the woods I had to walk past the big, open windows where the devotees were chanting *japa*. They saw me and I thought someone might come out and join me, but no, I broke loose and have come down the forest path. Yesterday on this path, I saw two snails with colored shells. Their brown and tan striations reminded me of tweed jackets.

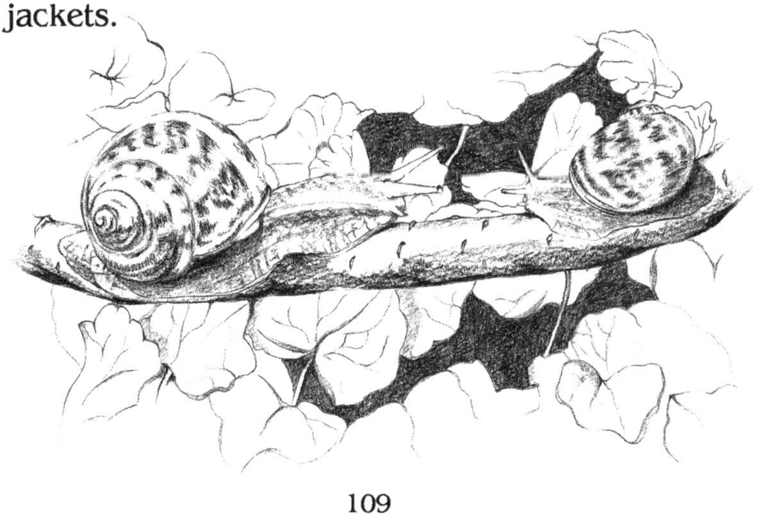

This is the time of the morning I usually spend preparing for *Śrīmad-Bhāgavatam* class, but I prepared earlier and I feel as ready as I'll ever be. The verse is about repentance. Ajāmila says, "What am I in comparison to the all-auspicious chanting of the holy names?" In the purport, Prabhupāda says we should always regret what we did in the past. I myself don't feel repentance, but I like to talk about it. What is repentance and why don't I feel it? I am attracted to the idea that by repentance, remorse, and reform, we can improve ourselves. Improvement is necessary.

Devotees hear they're supposed to be repentant, so they feel sorry because of some little mistake or some bad quality in their material character. Repentance, however, is something deeper. The dictionary defines repentance as anguish and remorse of a moral wrong. In one purport, Prabhupāda said we should feel repentance over the fact that we're acting separately from our constitutional position and trying to take the place of God.

I want to feel happy. I don't want to feel remorse. But it is a necessary stage, as Ajāmila experienced.

Because of my sinful activities in this life, I cannot think in pure Kṛṣṇa consciousness. I think of sex and material hang-ups, and so many other things. Real humility arising from regret can be a part of our character. It needn't conflict with the natural joy that comes in Kṛṣṇa consciousness. I haven't figured these things out, but I'll try to give them some expression in the *Bhāgavatam* class.

How nice it is that the woods are dense. I know even fewer birds here than I do in America, and if I ask devotees the names of birds, they just give me their French names. I miss the sound of the woodthrush, but I hear the crow. Crows are found everywhere.

This path leads past an open field covered by a carpet of bright yellow rape flowers. There are daisies here too, and purple wildflowers, and a few mushrooms. In the distance, I can see New Māyāpura's château, although it's partly obscured by the trees.

Farther along the path is a huge tree which forms a canopy over a large area. Inside the wall of branches is a room-like space where the children of New Māyāpura like to play. Whenever I read in the six Gosvāmīs' literature about Rādhā and Kṛṣṇa going to a *kuñja,* I think of this place. In Rādhā-Kṛṣṇa's pastimes, a *kuñja* might consist of several trees with a cottage standing among them, or it might be a natural cottage built from the tree itself. All the leaves of this tree point down, almost like those of a weeping willow. At first, I can't see the branches due to the covering leaves. The tree is a green shelter. In one place there is an opening, like a door, inviting me to enter.

Once inside, the whole thing looks like the canopy of a Ratha-yātrā cart, only much bigger. There's a hard earth floor with dried leaves scattered about, and across the floor the tree's massive roots spread. The great grey trunk itself divides into four main branches, which themselves are as thick and muscular as tree trunks.

These branches go up and branch out and then start to hang down. Some of the branches even touch the ground. It's similar to a banyan tree, but I don't know what kind of tree it is. It is the New Māyāpura *kuñja*. From one strong branch hangs a knotted rope for the children's swing. There's also a hole that the children have dug. Other than that, the *kuñja* doesn't look very used. It's a private place.

While I like to think of this tree as a *kuñja*, this place is not Vṛndāvana. In Vṛndāvana we can circumambulate trees, touch their roots, and offer them *ārati*, knowing that they are sacred living entities. We can't say that about trees in France. Of course, there's something special about the *dhāma* even in France. By kicking the earth I found three or four old garlands, as crackly and dry as fallen leaves. No doubt these garlands were offered to Rādhā-Govinda-Mādhava. Now they are here, at the base of this tree. The tree itself may not be an elevated living entity, but it is receiving mercy by being on the *dhāma*, Kṛṣṇa's place.

There are also some large feathers on the ground, but they are not peacock feathers as might be found at the base of Vṛndāvana trees.

If I were a devotee living in Vṛndāvana, I could take you on a tour of Rādhā-kuṇḍa and Śyāma-kuṇḍa. But it's nice here, isn't it? We can be together and speak our minds and still be only a five-minute walk from seeing the beautiful forms of Rādhā-Govinda-Mādhava.

It takes time to know the Deity when you've been away. Govinda-Mādhava doesn't stand very upright. He's bent over to the left and seems intoxicated in His dancing. He's glamorous. Rādhārāṇī is also dancing with Kṛṣṇa in that mood. It has taken me awhile to get past the external appearance and start to appreciate Their wholeness as *arcā-vigraha.* I realized this morning while singing at *maṅgala-ārati,* that we have to be charitable when we think of the devotees and the devotees' worship of the Deities. We have to simply see the good everyone is doing. That is the Vaiṣṇava vision, the Vṛndāvana vision. We are supposed to see all the residents of the *dhāma* as special.

If you were here, I think you too would warm up to the special beauty of Rādhā-Govinda-Mādhava. The devotees are fond of these Deities; I could sense it in their singing. It's a special and unexplained phenomenon how over months and years devotees develop real affection for their *arcā-vigrahas.* I like hearing them sing, "Jaya Kṛṣṇa-Balarāma, Jaya Kṛṣṇa-Balarāma" with that French accent on "Balarāma." When we get into the spirit of the community, we can taste their devotion.

I'm running out of time and paper, so I'm going to leave the *kuñja* and go back. As we cross the fields, watch out for the prickly weeds.

June 15
New Māyāpura
France

Dear fellow lecturers,

Today I thought I should try to write a more internal letter. Yesterday's letter was about the paths, *kuñja,* property, and Deities here at New Māyāpura. I wrote myself a note in the temple that today I should go to the *kuñja* and write to someone from there, but not a description of the walk. That was nice for one day, but now I have to go deeper.

I'm thinking about lectures and what they can convey to people about the Kṛṣṇa conscious philosophy. Lectures have their limitations—and these are related to the speaker's limits and the limits of his or her audience. The expert lecturer knows his audience and speaks to it in a way that will give the most benefit. However, he's not unnecessarily worried whether his audience will be pleased with his words. Kṛṣṇadāsa Kavirāja Gosvāmī says that if he worries how others will receive his writing, he will not be able to fullfill his purpose. He is praising Kṛṣṇa and repeating what he has heard from previous authorities. He is not trying to cater to the likes and dislikes of his readership. With this attitude, he produced the most powerful literature.

When I prepare to give *Bhāgavatam* class, I select powerful statements from the philosophy, but whether they'll be powerful when spoken by me I don't know. I never know. We may think our lecture was good, but it's effect may have come across as superficial. We may think our lecture was mediocre, yet it might have a lasting effect on someone. The duty of speaking has to be discharged sincerely, and if possible, with compassion. I think that's certainly more important than trying to be inspired or to give what we think is a dazzling performance. A dazzling performance is only surface charm. We have to speak with a real desire to be faithful to *paramparā*, and with faith that it will help people.

In other words, we can overdo the sense of personal compassion and personal reaching out. The mind is so tricky. We can even observe ourselves while lecturing and see our gestures are merely theatrical. We should speak simply, out of duty. If we want to help others, we should not desire a reward for our speaking.

Prabhupāda often discredits "professional reciters" who speak to get a reward or for prestige. Their lives are not renounced and they actually misuse the *Bhāgavatam* by dwelling on the sensational parts, like the *rāsa* dance, while exploiting their audience with oratorical skills. Prabhupāda's followers tend to think they are free from these speaking *anarthas*, but they may be present in subtle forms.

Today, for example, the topic of the verse is fall down from spiritual life. Ajāmila says he's determined not to fall down again; he's going to control his mind and senses. In the purport, Prabhupāda says we have to pray to Kṛṣṇa that we don't fall down. So I have outlined a few of these points on "Post-its" and attached them to the *Bhāgavatam* page. Surely I can get through a twenty or thirty-minute talk trusting in my God-given intelligence to recall points from *śāstra* that are relevant to the ISKCON community. Then the audience will raise questions (which I may regard as good or not so good), and without discrimination, I will try my best to answer them. It's a great privilege to be able to do this—to represent Vyāsadeva and to sit on the ISKCON *vyāsāsana* for *Śrīmad-Bhāgavatam* class. That's partly why I'm writing this letter—to think how to do it nicely and to try to escape *anarthas*.

In simpler terms, we want to give a lecture that will be interesting rather than a routine exposition of dogma. But there's a fine line between being interesting and giving a performance. Likewise, there's a fine line between being an unpretentious, *paramparā* teacher and a lackluster, boring speaker. After all, we are employing speaking skills. We are engaging in the art of oratory. We are trying to hold the audience's attention. We may have to use the methods any speaker would use: getting to the heart of the message, avoiding a long preamble, conveying, if possible, one simple message, and giving many concrete examples. These are standard methods used in the college classroom or in political speech-writing, and they can be used in the service of Kṛṣṇa.

And while it's good to try to help people, we should not be attached to a particular result. We should keep on speaking about Kṛṣṇa and how to practice Kṛṣṇa consciousness, taking every opportunity to glorify the Lord on the basis of *Śrīmad-Bhāgavatam* and the Bhaktivedanta purports. This is our life.

June 16
New Māyāpura

Dear friends,

I am writing from the *kuñja* in hopes that the *kuñja* itself will draw from me something I might wish to convey. As I entered, I noticed a big branch lying broken on the ground. I was here yesterday, but I didn't notice it. A friend told me that this tree is actually dead; only it's creepers are producing greenery. That's not true—the greenery belongs to the tree itself—but the way all the branches hang straight down, I have to wonder whether it's a sign that this tree is old and tired. The broken branch could have just broken off, or it could indicate something more serious.

Anyway, I didn't intend to talk about the branch; rather, I am asking for the *kuñja's* cooperation in helping me to write. O big tree, you have seen so many years. You have stood here tolerantly with your big knotty arms and your all-accepting breast. You are a very plain creature, dumb and suffering, yet you generously provide shade for others. While you don't live in Vṛndāvana, your good fortune has brought you to the property of the Hare Kṛṣṇa temple. Now you belong to Śrī Śrī Rādhā-Govinda-Mādhava, and sometimes you function indirectly in the devotees' activities.

I am here, trying to write a letter while sitting close to you. Maybe you and I can help each other in some way. I playfully call you a *kuñja*.

Thoughts of you bring to mind Rādhā-Kṛṣṇa's *kuñjas*. Each time I sing *nikuñja-yūno rati-keli-siddhyai* or even I talk about a *kuñja*, I think of you. Just as in the dictionary there's often a picture to illustrate a crossbow or an embroidery stitch, or some strange or obscure thing, so in the dictionary of my mind, a *kuñja* looks like you—a big area created by a tree which provides privacy from the outer world, just as a house does. You have served me in that way. Thank you.

But the fact is, we don't have entrance to the *kuñjas* in Vṛndāvana. We can walk around in this one and draw a few comparisons, but it's not possible to enter into the Vṛndāvana *kuñjas*. It might not even be possible in this lifetime.

By the mercy of the six Gosvāmīs, we are allowed to read about Kṛṣṇa's *kuñja* pastimes. The *Gurvaṣṭakam* says that the spiritual master is there assisting the *gopīs* as a maidservant. For example, in the morning after Rādhā and Kṛṣṇa's all-night pastimes, *mañjarīs* come in and sweep the *kuñja*. The *kuñja* may be strewn with crushed flowers and red *kuṅkuma*, broken bracelets and broken necklaces. The *mañjarīs* sweep all this up. At other times, they decorate the *kuñjas*, just as Vṛndā-devī decorates all of Vṛndāvana. Similarly, the maidservants decorate the *kuñjas* with garlands and aromatic incense. Sometimes it's so attractive that Rādhā and Kṛṣṇa will remark, "Who has decorated this *kuñja?*"

How fortunate is the tree who serves as a *kuñja!* Most fortunate of all are those who serve the *gopīs*, or who can at least hear about their service with spiritual greed.

Dear old tree of New Māyāpura-dhāma, I am just babbling at your roots, speaking in an unrealized way. I'm a dry and distant monk who chants alone, who cannot control his mind, and who has no real access to the *mādhurya* mysteries. I take it for granted that you have no access to them at all. So in that sense, we make a good team—we're both outsiders. You're a pretty good *kuñja* and I'm in a auspicious position because I can read and hear about *kuñja-līlā*. Yet we are both outsiders to the transcendental facts. Still, I yearn for the pastimes of Rādhā and Kṛṣṇa. I'm not satisfied to come here and swing back and forth on this rope like a child. By Prabhupāda's grace, I'm also liberated from wanting to do any kind of sinful activity in the *kuñja*. Maybe all I can do is daydream about something that will take place millions of years in the future for both you and me, dear tree.

I don't know how much longer you have to live, but at this present moment, you are draped with garlands from the Deities, and the devotees come here to chant the Hare Kṛṣṇa mantra. It may be possible for you and me to meet in the future as *kuñja* colleagues.

When will the day come when we can relish and qualify to read the books of the six Gosvāmīs? When will the day come when we will finally forget all mundane association with sexuality and become free enough to hear, without blushing, the love exchanges between the all-attractive Boy and the all-attractive Girl? When that day comes, all our austerities and good deeds will finally bear fruit.

Let no one try to enter the *kuñja* prematurely. (In Vṛndāvana, Lord Śiva as Gopīśvara prevents anyone from doing that.) Let no one dabble in these things for the wrong reason. But let us be aware of the goal and rid ourselves of mundane lust so that we can develop the *adhikārī* (qualification) to hear about Rādhā-Kṛṣṇa. Only then will we understand our relationship with our spiritual master, of whom Viśvanātha Cakravartī says, "He is always engaged in the *kuñjas* of Vṛndāvana, assisting the *gopīs* who are arranging for the conjugal pastimes of Rādhā-Kṛṣṇa."

Part Two

Letters from Wicklow

July 3
Wicklow, Ireland

Dear friends,

I'm certainly glad to be here. I'm writing this letter at the beginning of what seems to be a very auspicious and happy time. I have planned to stay at a devotee's cottage here in Wicklow to study and write. From my point of view, this is a kind of paradise on earth. I just hope I can use the time well.

Wicklow is a very nice place. Being in Ireland means I can take a good walk. People don't get up so early, at least in this vicinity, and no dogs bother me. The road is fairly level. It's a narrow, tar-topped road bordered on either side by walls of greenery. Beyond the riotous weeds and wildflowers are rolling green pastures spotted with cows. The scene is pastoral—one of low-lying hills, stone walls, and an ever-moving sky. At one point there is a bridge that crosses a small stream. It rained all day yesterday, and all night, so there's a fresh, strong current in the stream. The rushing water makes a pleasant sound.

One of the features of my morning walks is solitude, but being alone is a kind of illusion. The *Bhagavad-gītā* says that if something is only temporary, it is *asat,* illusion. So this getting away to be alone is illusion. Actually, I don't claim to be alone. As I walk there are cows by the fence. Some of them eyed me curiously. And all the July greenery is bursting out on both sides of the road.

Living creatures are everywhere, but aside from them there is Kṛṣṇa, the Supreme Personality of Godhead. And Kṛṣṇa Himself, as Prabhupāda says, is not alone; just as a king comes with his entourage, so Kṛṣṇa comes with His associates when He enters this world.

An aspiring devotee like me likes to go out alone sometimes because too much mixing with people and too many demands make it difficult to remember those you really want to be with. I believe someone said that in solitude, you can pick your own company; that is, you can think of those people whose company you want to share. That's a good definition.

The people with whom we are obliged to spend time often talk about things we don't always care to hear. Invariably, people are troubled, and there is nothing much you can do for them except hear them out and suggest to them what you are trying to do yourself: surrender to Kṛṣṇa. You want to help, of course, but there is not much you can do.

So being alone, even temporarily, is something that I very much like. When I'm "alone" I try to think of Rādhā and Kṛṣṇa and what Prabhupāda has instructed. For example, this morning while chanting *japa* I was able to look at the picture of Rādhā and Kṛṣṇa. I was not alone; I was focused on Them.

They say the weather has been nice for the past two months—hardly any rain. But wouldn't you know it? Now it's raining and the sky is dark. It's summer, so the sky usually lightens early. It's wonderful, isn't it? These mornings of early light come at no other time of the year. It's such a luxury. And the trick to appreciating all these wonderful things is not to fall into sense gratification, but to serve Kṛṣṇa in every situation, taking whatever is there and using it in His service.

Although this is a season of early light and precious days, the winter has it's special features too, like the appetite you have for hot meals and the quietness of the snow. But if I had my choice, I would take this season of early light and wildflowers.

I returned from my walk to a little desk that my host has provided. It's one of those secretary desks that fold out, not really enough for a writer who gathers so many books around him and spreads out notebooks and manuscripts and other desk clutter. At least the desk is solid, not shaky. And there's a desk lamp. After my walk I sit here trying to express to you something of my experience.

My hope is that through writing I might come to see better. I don't refer just to physical sight. (My physical sight is not very good and, to make matters worse, raindrops splatter the "windshield" of my glasses.) Rather, I refer to something else—being able to see within, to uncover what cannot be seen, to be a little more daring, perhaps, and honest, and let the yearnings come out. I hope by walking up and down the road and returning to this desk to express to you what I feel, I'll be able to see things more clearly and improve my service to guru and Kṛṣṇa.

July 4
Wicklow

Dear friends,

I've been out walking in the rain. It's a beautiful experience having raindrops bounce off your raincoat while you're all alone under a gray, dawning sky. I stopped to bask in the freshness of everything, to bask in the solitude. I wondered who I would write to today. Shall I write to the tree, the one with the heavy broken branch? Should I write to Prabhupāda? But the feelings I have for Prabhupāda right now seem too deep to put into words. So I chose to write to my friends.

But what do I want to say? I want to say this: it was raining and now it has stopped, and I have been out walking in it. Surely a friend can appreciate that this is vital communication. We go to our friends to share good things and for help in bad times. My friends are Kṛṣṇa conscious devotees; we share Kṛṣṇa consciousness. I hope that we can achieve our *param-gati,* our final goal of direct service to Kṛṣṇa in the spiritual world. I hope to see Kṛṣṇa even now, looking with my eyes, my God-given eyes, at the hills and the sky. This letter is my way of saying hello to a friend, wherever he or she may be. Waving to each other over distances, confirming the like-mindedness of Kṛṣṇa consciousness among friends.

As I walked home, I saw the stretch of road leading to the cottage and wanted to cover it as best I could. It's not only a physical distance, but also a stretch of time. The sky was beginning to lighten and I wanted to take advantage of the moment. Communication isn't the only way to use time, but it's a way that I know. I strive to communicate, but behind the communication is the subtle desire to be more in love and more awake and more alive to the beauty and protection of Kṛṣṇa. We are usually half-dead, just coasting. Communication, even though we may talk about so many things, tends to sound like idle pleasantries because what we really want to say is I wish I loved Kṛṣṇa. Is it possible that by talking with you I can increase my attachment to Kṛṣṇa? And is it possible that you too can be drawn closer to Kṛṣṇa? I want to use my time in the best way possible, and the best way is to talk about Kṛṣṇa.

As a person who reads letters, I sometimes become impatient if somebody talks about too many ordinary, external things. Now those things may be sweet and personal and written in a mood of sharing, but I find it hard to spare the time. Why then, do I try to foist this external and sometimes lengthy correspondence on you? My other correspondents expect me to respond point for point and as soon as possible. But I don't mind if you don't read these letters for months or even years, and you never need to answer them. The letters are there for you to pick up whenever you want. As interested friends, you have told me that you want to hear whatever is going on with me, just like a mother does, or a close relative.

How are you, my friends? I hope you're practicing Kṛṣṇa consciousness in your own sphere, not feeling too lonely or too attracted by *māyā*. You have your day; I have my day. We may seem far away from each other, but we can be connected by service. We can chant and depend on Kṛṣṇa and get enlightenment from the same source, so there's no need to be lonely in the sense of feeling bereft.

What is it we want most? What will nourish us? The *śāstras* say it's to associate with Kṛṣṇa in a loving way, to try to please His senses. That may seem like distant theology instead of a solution to immediate concerns, but we shouldn't take it that way. The immediate emotional needs we have may be misguided to some degree, if we're expecting too much from a marriage or even a friendship. But these relationships, including our relationship and correspondence, can be fulfilling when we help each other and point each other to the goal. We have some purpose together which is enduring. Therefore, I'm saying that relationships are significant, but they have to have Kṛṣṇa at the center, because then we can actually be close.

I remember Prabhupāda picking up the phone in his apartment in 1966 and talking to a *yogī* named Yogi Dankara. Prabhupāda said, "Yes, I love you too, but not this skin love." That phrase stuck in my mind. The love we want to offer to each other is not this skin love.

Skin love is based on a false premise. It's outrageous, in fact, because in order to experience sex pleasure with a person, I have to take the part of Kṛṣṇa Himself and try to be the enjoyer, the connoisseur of *rasa*, the debauche, the stealer of other men's wives. These are all Kṛṣṇa's prerogatives, not mine. This behavior is bad enough in a *mūḍha,* but it's much worse in a devotee. If after regularly hearing that Kṛṣṇa is the *ādi-puruṣa* a devotee still acts pervertedly, then he's not a devotee. Bhaktivinoda Ṭhākura says such a devotee may wear neck beads, but he's actually a *kālīchela,* a devotee-servant of Kālī.

I reach out to you, dear friends, not in an abstract way and not in a role as teacher, but in love, based on our nourishing each other in love for Kṛṣṇa.

Let me close by saying I'm glad you are there and that we can share a spiritual affection. This satisfies some undeniable need we have. Then, being a bit more *ātmārāma,* when we go to the scriptures and hear their high call for renunciation and devotion to the Supreme, we'll be better able to follow. We won't think that we first have to get some love in some other way. And whatever we do learn and feel from the scriptures, we can share.

July 7
Wicklow

Dear friends,

At this time of the year, it's light by 4:30 A.M. and I am out by 5:00. There are usually dark Kṛṣṇa-colored clouds hanging low, sometimes half-obscuring the rounded hills. It's hard to call them mountains, although on the map they're called the Wicklow Mountains. They are definitely hills, rounded like upturned bowls. This morning above the hills and very dark clouds, there was a pearly blue sky. It was a very nice, cool, summer morning. On my right as I walked along the narrow, tar-topped road, were freshly cut fields with piles of grass lying here and there. The pastures are fenced with a few barbed wire strands and often from the strands hang tufts of sheep's wool. If you go over and touch it, the wool is fine and white and damp with dew.

I take these walks after an intensive few hours of writing and chanting. It's like coming out of *kṛṣṇa-bhajana* into nature, and this may be a way of accounting for why my thoughts as I walk when I write you do not dwell on the scriptures and Vraja. But I hope those things are never far from my mind and that the scenes I like to relate to you are a kind of setting in which to breathe and live in Kṛṣṇa consciousness. Śrīla Prabhupāda wanted us to take Vṛndāvana all over the world. For him, Vṛndāvana was any place where we could think of Kṛṣṇa and serve Him. And he wanted to spread that mood in preaching.

As I walked up the road, I approached the pride and joy of the Wicklow devotee community—their new schoolhouse. It's not a big building—just one story with four windows across the front and very plain, like Irish buildings tend to be. A car was parked outside and a light shone from the windows. Maybe the teacher, Prabhupāda dāsa, is living there and chanting his *japa* in the early morning hours. There are about eighteen devotees living in the Wicklow area. Each family has their own little house. They don't have an ISKCON temple per se, but they are all devotees of Prabhupāda. They've built a schoolhouse and now have their own teacher.

On the intersection near the schoolhouse is a sign posted by the Irish army: "Warning—Danger. Notice of firing in progress in the glen of Immal will be indicated by the display of a red flag by day and red light by night at this point. Thereafter, in accordance with Section 274 Defense Acts, 1954, all movement east of here is prohibited. It is dangerous to enter the army ranges at any time. Any person finding a projectile or any part of a projectile is warned not to touch it, but advised to report it's location to the range warden or the nearest guard station." This morning when I was out, an olive drab army jeep stopped and soldiers posted a red flag. I determined by the rising sun that I was heading east, so my customary turn would take me either north or south. As I was making these calculations, I turned and saw Prabhupāda dāsa looking out at me from the school window. I was a little embarrassed that he should see me in my rubber coat, but I guess he'll have to get used to it.

Magpies joined me in my retreat from the army range. Do you know what a magpie looks like? They are large birds, about the size of crows, and their black and white markings make them look like they're wearing tuxedos, something like penguins. A couple of magpies landed on a nearby stone wall. In Ireland, stone walls are made by placing one stone on another often with no mortar between them. These walls have been put up with great labor and they separate one pasture from another. Much of the land is like that—green meadows and rolling hills, with stone walls running through them. You can hear the lowing of cows, which would make for an idyllic setting except for the fact that the cows are raised for slaughter. If, as in Kṛṣṇa's kingdom, cows were raised to give milk and the milk used for butter and yogurt, then that would be wonderful. But Ireland is the European Economic Community's supplier of "livestock."

I feel awkward using the words "European Economic Community." I prefer to talk about Vraja, Yāvaṭ, Saṅkeṭ. In fact, I probably know more about Vraja than I do about the European Economic Community and this becomes obvious when I slide into worldly references with other devotees. One night in Dublin I gave a class about *kṛṣṇa-kathā*. I told some pastimes. By way of introduction, I explained how we hesitate to talk about Kṛṣṇa because it seems beyond us, mythological. I myself was hesitating, but once I started, I felt better and spoke about the Kāliya pastimes. Afterwards, in the question and answer period, a devotee said, "You advocated that we should talk among ourselves about Kṛṣṇa, but it's hard to do. We sometimes feel that we're not so advanced or that it's *sahajiyā* if we try to talk about Kṛṣṇa. How can we do it if it's not natural for us?"

I told him, "Even if it's not natural, just begin. Like the engine in your car on a cold winter day, if you crank it up, it will start to hum. It'll be nice, once you get started, so you have to practice." And I suggested that they do so at designated times. This is why Prabhupāda established the *Bhāgavatam* class every morning. Also, in our own schedule we should have a time set aside every day for reading and talking about Kṛṣṇa.

And this is how it goes. I write you spontaneously about magpies and the view and being excited about the red army flag and becoming startled by using a worldly term like "European

Economic Community"—which brings me back to Kṛṣṇa. It's a roundabout introduction, but at least we're steering toward Kṛṣṇa.

And if you want to be as direct as possible, without preambles, then do as I am about to do and immediately chant: Hare Kṛṣṇa Hare Kṛṣṇa, Kṛṣṇa Kṛṣṇa Hare Hare/Hare Rāma Hare Rāma, Rāma Rāma Hare Hare. I hope you too are chanting Hare Kṛṣṇa soon and often. Of course, when we do chant, we won't always be able to blot out distractions. We will still get excited when we see a hare jump in front of our path and we'll still wonder about the names of those little white flowers that look about ready to turn into blackberries. (Are they blackberries?) But we can return to chanting and try to remember all-attractive Kṛṣṇa. Everything is Kṛṣṇa, and especially His name, who takes away everyone's inauspicious distractions and gives us, instead, His very self.

July 8
Wicklow

Dear friends,

I would like to address letters to different persons, but it seems too much like an uninspiring duty. I have to write so many regular letters, why not write another one? I could write a letter to some young girls in Dublin who are interested in Kṛṣṇa consciousness, but who have some opposition from their parents. There are so many letters I could write, but I don't feel like it.

Dear friends, today I took a walk in a different direction. After passing one farmhouse without waking any dogs, I thought I would be well secluded walking down a narrow road hedged on either side by greenery. On one side was a fence and gate leading into a pasture. A muddy puddle by the gate reflected a patch of sky. Further on, evergreens lined both sides of the path, so I had a sense of going deeper into the green, deeper into the solitude.

Somehow as I walked I was reminded of the past—a visit I made to Ireland a few years ago when I was trying to enter a life of prayer. Things seem quite different now. I am more fixed on the goal of Kṛṣṇa in Vṛndāvana. Yet I was fervent on that previous visit, and the walks I took helped me to go deeper.

It's nice to walk in silence. Today I walked up to a large herd of cows—maybe fifty or sixty or more. They were almost all black and white, and many of them had big milk bags, like the cows at Gītā-nāgarī. Some of them got nervous as I walked by. I too felt nervous, thinking that a herdsman might not be far off. After all, it was 5:00 A.M. Someone might be coming to milk them and that would change the whole mood of my walk. Alone I could see the cows, feel sympathy for them, and think of them as beautiful. I could see Kṛṣṇa's miracle—how these peaceful animals eat grass and produce milk for human beings. But if the herdsman came, I would suspect that he was wondering who was this person walking around idly in the early morning? Then he might see my *tilaka* and say, "It's a Hare Kṛṣṇa. They have some crazy philosophy about cow protection. Maybe he's going to let my cows out or do something to my herd." I didn't want to linger, but walked past the cows, came to the end of the pasture, and started back, chanting my *japa* all the while.

I stopped at one place along the road because I heard the sound of water and found a tiny creek, run-off caused by the recent rains. I leaned against the fence and looked at the water running over the rocks. I thought I had found the peace and solitude I was seeking on this walk, but then I began to compare it to Vṛndāvana. What is this peace I think I've found here? It's not saturated with Vṛndāvana *līlā*. Vṛndāvana is noisy and populated, but it's saturated with Kṛṣṇa's pastimes.

Of course, no place is perfect until you become perfect, until you become satisfied and Kṛṣṇa conscious. Otherwise, even when the surroundings are peaceful, you cannot be loving or absorbed in Kṛṣṇa. Or, if you go to the place of Kṛṣṇa's loving pastimes, Vṛndāvana, you will be distracted by its foreign exterior. At any rate, I don't think I could be satisfied to live in a place like Ireland all my life, and to spend peaceful days in prayer. Not now that I realize everything is so connected to Kṛṣṇa in Vṛndāvana. To be so far away from Him, to make a deliberate place here, where the land is not His land, except in a general sense, would seem artificial.

The only way devotees can live in different parts of the world is to preach. Then if they are fully practicing Kṛṣṇa consciousness, the country in which they live becomes their *prabhu-datta-deśa*. For example, even when devotees farm, it's a kind of preaching, and the land itself becomes their service. But with me, just to walk and think poetic thoughts and write them down is not enough reason to be in exile from places that are more inherently Kṛṣṇa conscious. So my present practice of traveling to temples to preach with occasional breaks during which I can take walks and write is nice. But it's also nice to go to Vṛndāvana, which I will do in a month.

What about you, friends? What combination of places and services is best for you? Take a break and think about it, and let me know what you're planning. Then try to work toward it so that you get the most satisfying combination for serving Kṛṣṇa according to time, place, and person.

July 9
Wicklow

Dear friends,

It's raining and again I've been out walking. I have told you something of where I am. I've rooted myself, starting with bodily sensations and descriptions of the countryside knowing that you, as friends, are pleased to hear these things. Communication is like that. First come the preliminary topics, then later we enter into a deeper exchange.

This morning it's cooler. Uddhava dāsa, at whose house we're staying, said that in this area, even in the middle of the summer, there might be a winter-like day. So it's cold, rainy, and I have an attack of hay fever or something. While walking I heard the loud bleating of sheep. They don't seem happy either, but I am happy to be practicing Kṛṣṇa consciousness, even in the rain.

This morning the narrow, tar-covered road was two shiny tracks, almost like railroad tracks, where the rain had collected. Down the middle is a green row of grass that has somehow grown through the tar. Grass can be all-pervading. Prabhupāda even used it as an example. He said that when you see grass growing on the sidewalk, it means that somehow a soul has been given an opportunity to enter there. The seed is looking for a chance to sprout anywhere, and here it pops up in the middle of this old country road, making one long row as far as you can see. Because of the rain, the long low hills are partly obscured and I could almost see the rain as one big covering cloud. So it is.

Yesterday I mentioned how we each have to find our combination of duties and personal tendencies. We can't say that we'll only do what we're inclined to do. We're meant to fulfill duty; we become happy in duty. Another way to put it is we need a variety of activities to make us satisfied. Eventually we'll come to the point where there will be no duty—meaning, no prescribed orders—but we will feel more personally absorbed in loving service to Kṛṣṇa. Others may see us as doing our duty. They may see us as responsible and as contributing members of the community, or they may not. The fact is, a devotee who follows the inclination of his heart to serve Kṛṣṇa is contributing best to society, because he is driven only by the desire to serve Kṛṣṇa and thus he teaches people the most important duty in this material world.

I don't know if this is making sense to you, but I'm talking about spontaneous devotional service and about personal satisfaction and trying to hint to you that you should find your own. Much of it has to do with placing chanting and hearing as priorities in your life. I have to leave it to you because I can't dictate to anyone how they should bring this about. It might me irresponsible of me. I have to be daring enough to tell the plain truth—that chanting and hearing are most important. You have to sort it out in terms of your other duties.

Śāstra, you might say, is radical in the way things are stated. For example, one verse says that a person who has surrendered to Kṛṣṇa and is serving Him has no other duties, not to the demigods, family, forefathers, or society. No other duties. So you have to determine the proper balance for your own life. Abandoning all other duties is irresponsible until the time comes when you are fully surrendered to Kṛṣṇa. But how are you going to fully surrender to Kṛṣṇa? You must begin by surrendering.

I didn't know this letter would become so preachy; I hope you don't mind, because we're friends. We're not ordinary friends, like friends in the world, are we? We look forward to forceful exchanges of doctrine.

I must tell you of something that happened on my walk. I came to a meadow in which there were two huge horses. I was shocked at how big they were. They looked so big that they seemed like horses from a dream—fearful. I thought they were statues at first. One of them was brown with a white *tilaka* marking down his nose, and the other was brown with white legs. It seemed as though they could walk right out the gate if they wanted. One horse did begin to walk, so I began to walk away quickly in case he decided to come through the gateway. Then he stopped, after a few steps, and started chewing at the grass in the rain. That's one thing about Ireland: there is plenty of rain and the grass is always coming up and the beasts are always chewing at it.

The idea of being irresponsible in one's duty reminds me that a preacher has to be careful even in the tone and manner in which he speaks. Recently at a public meeting a woman asked me, are there times when an initiated devotee may not be able to chant his or her rounds? I took it to mean that she was referring to motherhood and how hard it is to chant when raising children. So I answered that somehow or other, we have to always chant sixteen rounds. Now I don't think I was wrong in saying that, but I said it with a kind of flourish that had in it the privilege of *sannyāsa.* I said that this practice of *bhakti* is the most important thing in life and it shouldn't be neglected in the name of taking care of a family. Rather, the duty of caring for a family is not mentioned in the nine items of *bhakti;* it's not even one of the sixty-four items of devotional service. I think that remark was a little startling, so some people in the audience laughed.

Later, during a group discussion, the topic of my exchange with the woman was introduced. There was even discussion about why the audience laughed. Did they laugh out of nervousness? Did they laugh because they wanted to make fun of the woman with the child? Did they support neglecting children? I was accused of being an old-style, heavy-handed *sannyāsī* who has no sympathy for the realities of child-rearing. It became a big thing.

I want to take the blame for being insensitive in making my point. If I had just been simple and not added so much flourish to my answer, it would have been better. This is an indication that a preacher has to be responsible, not only for telling the truth, but also for the way in which he tells it.

Perhaps the better response would have been to say one has to figure out how to do both. You cannot neglect your child, nor can you neglect the vow you made to your spiritual master to chant sixteen rounds. It's better to present the problem as one each person must solve. Again, every individual is responsible for his or her own life.

This goes back to my point that I have to leave the choice of surrender to you. Some things are difficult for us to bear and they sound too radical and too harsh. A *sādhu* is supposed to cut, but he has to be careful too. He preaches to people who are not prepared for much renunciation. If a speaker has no sensitivity to their situation, how much does he want to preach? There has to be a balance. When people are unable to follow everything, the preacher must be sympathetic, but he cannot compromise the message. So the message is: find your way, and if that is to be Kṛṣṇa conscious, all emphasis must be given to chanting and hearing.

July 10
Wicklow

Dear friends,

Every day is delightful in its own way, if we can only see how Kṛṣṇa is manifesting ways for us to approach Him. In the opening chapters of *Śrīmad-Bhāgavatam* we are told that attraction to the message of Kṛṣṇa is the real goal of life, otherwise our activities are *śrama eva hi kevalam,* useless labor. Sense gratification should be minimized and we should inquire about Kṛṣṇa. We are very fortunate to be attracted to the message of Kṛṣṇa, because that message will dissolve all dirty things in the heart.

Materialists have no idea what is being said here, because it is not possible for them to think of a goal of life other than sense gratification. But by Prabhupāda's grace we understand the spiritual goal of being attracted to Kṛṣṇa.

What an ideal and luxuriant combination, to sit at a desk and read the message of Kṛṣṇa and then go out into a beautiful morning. As I said, every morning is delightful, but some are especially so. And they're made more delightful by the variety. Today the rain has stopped. In the west, there are cloud banks, but they only go up a few layers and then the sky is clear blue. In the east the horizon is whitish, which means the sun is coming, that great event which takes place every day. And for us, even sunrise is a personal manifestation of God's glories. The daily appearance Of the sun signifies the sungod has become powerful by his worship of the energy of Kṛṣṇa, namely Śrīmatī Rādhārāṇī, so it is by Her grace that all the worlds are effulgent.

Today is Ekādaśī, and tomorrow at the schoolhouse I will give the first of a series of weekly classes for the six or so devotee families in the Wicklow area. In Dublin on two occasions I spoke about the importance of reading the *śāstras* and I'm going to continue with that theme. I found some nice verses from *Bhāgavatam*, which are quoted in the *Bhakti-sandarbha*, about the importance of hearing. I don't want to overdo it, but my guess is that the householders here don't do much reading. They're probably busy raising children or building and repairing their houses or taking care of their gardens or of course working to earn money for all this—so when do they have the time? I want to encourage them as a friend to read more so they might develop a taste for reading.

Prabhupāda was so positive with us, asking that we just add Kṛṣṇa. What is the problem? It is not difficult. You can just chant Hare Kṛṣṇa. You can hear about Kṛṣṇa. Ultimately I will be speaking encouragement to myself. When we have time and attention we should read from *śāstra* whatever interests us so that gradually our attraction for reading will grow. I don't want to browbeat them, but I do want to talk about hearing. I could even tell them about methods of reading together and how enlivening it is.

After promoting the importance of hearing, I thought we could enter directly into Kṛṣṇa's pastimes. I plan to read to the *gṛhasthas* from *Kṛṣṇa* book, beginning where the cowherd boys go to the wives of the *brāhmaṇas* and ask them to please give some food for Kṛṣṇa. The wives respond quickly and take their preparations to Kṛṣṇa, personally seeing the beautiful vision of Him in the woods. We read in *Caitanya-bhāgavata* that when that verse was read, it produced ecstasy. Kṛṣṇa speaks to the wives and tells them to go home. He says they will develop greater attraction to Him in that way than if they followed their proposal to stay with Him.

As I walked along this morning, I continually saw rabbits on the road ahead of me. They would never let me walk directly up to them, but I would see sometimes as many as three or four, very little ones and bigger ones, gamboling on the road in front of me. When I got too close they would jump into the weeds and brush at the edge of the road. Now, in July, the roadside is so thick with bushes and tasseled weeds and wildflowers and briar patches that the rabbits soon become hidden. My guess is that they really didn't run very far into the brush, but sat and waited until I had gone by and then came out again.

On early morning walks, no one else is up and it's almost like I'm the "emperor" of all I see. Now, I don't want to be an emperor to dictate or rule over this vast domain before my eyes, but there's nobody but me to pray to Kṛṣṇa, to offer everything I see to Kṛṣṇa. Today everything seems so bright, and in the distance you can see houses and the windows in the houses. You suspect that the people are up because it's already so bright out. It's so beautiful I wondered how people could remain indoors, what to speak of sleeping, on a morning like this. They could be out here looking at the long-stemmed foxglove, whose flowers look like violet jewels in this light. Some anonymous persons have named them foxglove, as if the foxes could put their paws into them and wear them as gloves. Shining on the stem of one of them were two big drops of dew. Looking over a little hillock I saw a rabbit who was not even bothering to take shelter from my intrusion. Who would want to stay in bed and miss that?

The ideal, however, is not just to come out here and practice nature worship, but to read the beautiful *Bhāgavatam*, see the picture of Kṛṣṇa playing the flute and dancing with Śrīmatī Rādhārāṇī, hear from Śukadeva Gosvāmī about the importance of hearing, and then go out into the fresh air. If you're fortunate you can take with you, in your mind, *ślokas* like *śṛṇvatāṁ sva-kathāḥ kṛṣṇaḥ puṇya-śravaṇa-kīrtanaḥ* or the Gopal mantra, *klīṁ kṛṣṇāya govindāya gopī-jana-vallabhāya svāhā.* And on top of all this fortune, you are even more fortunate if you have friends of whom you're thinking.

You're grateful to Kṛṣṇa that the medium of perceiving these wonders is your own body. You're aware that health comes and goes, and you're even somewhat aware that the body is temporary and death is not so far away. But still

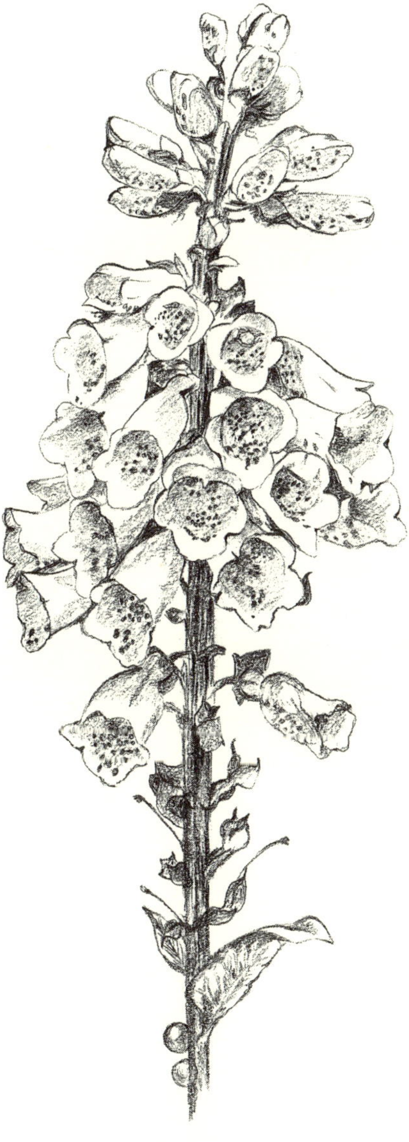

you're thankful for this present occasion when you're healthy enough to walk, to breathe, and to exercise your limbs in such a nice natural setting with *kṛṣṇa-kathā* fresh in your mind. All these activities are done through the body and the mind, which are given to us by Kṛṣṇa. So you celebrate those instruments also: the eyes and their ability to see so freshly, the body's ability to propel you along, swinging legs and hips, rhythmic motions of the head and neck, beating heart—all are gifts from the Lord. If used rightly these needn't be the cause of entanglement, but a way to propel us into spiritual life.

July 11
Wicklow

Dear friends,

Wouldn't you know it? After one sunny morning, it's again rainy. I looked out the window at first light and thought there were no clouds at all, but then I noticed there was no blue, only clouds. So I ventured out and it began misting.

I like the opportunity to be able to speak with you, and regularly. It's a kind of continual feast for me in that regard, because for weeks and months at a time I'm not able to write these letters. So let me not hold back.

As I was leaving the cottage today, our friend Prabhupāda dāsa was alone in a darkened room chanting his *japa*. I think he was pretty much awake. His chanting was a droning monotone, but there was something very steady and persistent about it. I had just been upstairs reading a letter he had written me. Instead of going to Dublin he's staying with us this weekend, but he wrote that he was feeling anxiety that he wasn't out on the street distributing books, as is his custom. So I appreciate his determination and dedication to distribute books. I was thinking maybe his *japa* gets its steadiness from that austerity. And I was also thinking how much of our *japa* sounds joyless.

As for myself, I have to admit my chanting this morning didn't have the steadiness I heard in Prabhupāda dāsa's chanting. I was actually falling asleep during at least one round. And the very first rounds I chanted were interrupted by "great ideas." You know what that's like. There I was with all the paraphernalia—votive candles on the altar—and not even halfway through the first round I had a "great" idea for editing my writings. So I had to stop and write a note to my editor. I'm saying this in a half-jesting way, although I know it's a serious thing. I think it is a foible I share with most devotees. But if we could associate with more serious and more joyful *japa* chanters and become more aware of the overwhelming glories of *nāma-saṅkīrtana* and *japa* specifically, maybe we could do something more productive than joke about our foibles. This seems like something worth writing to you about and hearing your response.

But maybe I'm offering something of a utopian solution, that we should find some *japa mahātmā* and associate with him. The one or two times I found a very advanced *japa* chanter, he mostly kept the chanting to himself. I find that when my chanting gets really bad I'm indulging in distracted thoughts, and that's when I have no recourse but to put on Prabhupāda's *japa* tape. One Godbrother told me that we must remember the *japa* tape by Prabhupāda is a kind of public performance. It was recorded in the temple room during an initiation ceremony, so he was demonstrating *japa* to an audience of beginning devotees. Nevertheless, it is potent and so many of us depend on it to sustain us from our indulgence in distracted thoughts.

One thought I indulged in this morning was about baseball. I'll share this just to expose my folly. I have no real attraction to baseball. I have been out of touch with baseball for so long that I have very little idea of who the teams are and no idea of who the players are. What I was thinking about was the past—the 1951 National League playoffs between the Brooklyn Dodgers and the New York Giants. Little blips passed through my mind of the Giants' stadium at the Polo Grounds and the Dodgers' at Ebbetts Field, how the Giants won the first game and the Dodgers the second, and the third game was for the pennant.

It's so stubborn of us, so tamasic, so wasteful to dwell on distracted thoughts instead of putting conscious effort into hearing the holy names. Was there really any enjoyment in my thinking about the old baseball memory? No. And was there any benefit? No. But I did it, and one continues to do such things. We either chew the chewed from thirty or forty years ago, or come up with "great" ideas in the middle of our rounds.

One thing is clear: When our chanting is at this low level, when we chant just to get the rounds done, it's a sure sign of the low level of our Kṛṣṇa consciousness. At least it can make us humble, but it also should signal to us that we have to do something. I hope talking about these things is not another kind of wasteful indulgence, but that it will be an act of reform. I pray to Kṛṣṇa again, please let me pay attention to the holy names.

The few rounds I chanted outdoors this morning were a little better. At least there was no danger of falling asleep. But then as usual, the subtle material organ (called the mind) wanted to do many things instead of paying attention to the sweet personal names of the Lord. Śukadeva Gosvāmī says it's a materialistic man who thinks of many things instead of Kṛṣṇa. Such is our state.

When things come to the mind during *japa,* we don't even think of them as distractions. So while I was chanting, a fox appeared on the little narrow road in front of me and then ran into the bushes. I began thinking about him. What if he hadn't been afraid? What if he had confronted me? Then this led me to think of an article I had seen in a newsletter from the ISKCON farm in Śaraṇāgati about bears. A devotee described at length how a bear kept coming around his house and what he did to scare him. He finally opened the door and let out a scream from the bottom of his being and the bear became scared and ran away. So the train of thought goes from one thing to another. How far away it goes. The way to solve this, the only way, is to attain actual attraction and devotion in *prema.*

The *ācāryas* say that *prema* can be compared to ice whereas mechanical chanting is compared to water. You can put any substance into water and water will allow it to enter. But ice is so thick that it cannot be easily penetrated. So in that sense *prema* has to be a solid emotion, a solid concentration. Then, even when some memory of 1951 baseball playoffs wants to enter, or the sighting of a fox prompts the mind to think of something about bears, these things will just bounce off and not enter the solid *prema* meditation. In the meantime, we can at least try to post a guard outside our shaky meditation chamber and give him the orders to chase away these unwanted guests.

July 12
Wicklow

Dear friends,

Before I started on the walk today I looked out the window and it seemed very windy. During these summer nights it never seems to get entirely dark and I could see the tops of trees shaking violently, so I thought, I'm in for a windy walk. But when I started out, the wind had died down. Very low clouds were pushing over the tops of the hills so that I could only very faintly see the outline of the hilltop, and then not at all. I got the feeling that the clouds could blow away and the sky could clear momentarily. But in Ireland it's just one weather front after another, and within half an hour it can go from sun to cloud to sun again.

I don't know why I should tell you about the weather. I like to do it and hope you like to hear it. And that reminds me, I wish you would write me back more regularly. It seems like months (and it actually is about three months) since I've heard from you and I assume you're getting my letters, so please reply in kind.

Yesterday I was talking about *japa*. But thinking back, it seemed mostly talk about bad *japa*, and I felt a little ashamed today to think I had written like that. Prabhupāda writes in a purport that devotees are like scientists who exchange the results of their research. One gets the idea that these exchanges should be marked by some degree of expertise. I suppose the exchanges of the elevated devotees, like the six Gosvāmīs, are actually on the level of eternal *śāstra.* So I felt sorry that my talk was mostly about struggle. But this is our life. We don't like the struggles themselves, or that which holds us back from Kṛṣṇa consciousness. What we like is Kṛṣṇa consciousness. But our reality is one of struggle, so we honestly and hopefully talk about our level of Kṛṣṇa consciousness, even if it includes struggle. In fact, our imperfection is such that if we so much as notice we're neglectful and inattentive, it's a gain over the usual state of complacent mechanical ritual. Isn't it so?

Anyway, I felt ashamed and thought today I would write something more positive about *japa.* But to speak something more positive I'll have to turn to *śāstra.* Yesterday we were reading the *Śikṣāmṛta* and considering the glories of the holy name. Rūpa Gosvāmī has written that the Lord has two forms: His name and His transcendental body. He gives two Sanskrit words for it—*vākya* and *vācha.* But he says of the two forms the *vākya,* the voice form, is more merciful, because Kṛṣṇa is so accessible in the sound vibration of His name.

There are no hard and fast rules for chanting. In any contaminated condition we're encouraged to chant. And Lord Caitanya is so kind that after glorifying the power and purity of the holy name in his first verse *(ceto darpaṇa mārjanaṁ),* He says, "Although the chanting is so wonderful, as I've just described, yet I fail to appreciate the taste of the holy name." In His humility, the Lord entered that mood to show compassion for us who are struggling devotees. He was not endorsing the state of neglectful, inattentive chanting. He was pointing out that if we are on that low stage, we are still not without His mercy. He remembers us and He's encouraging us. He likes it that we persist, but the inattention and indulgence are not pleasing to Him. He's willing to forgive our faults. He sees that a person is trying and trying and trying, and seemingly getting nowhere.

Aside from my own immediate experiences of observing my mind and noticing my inattention, I feel more hopeful when I can repeat Lord Caitanya's words and be aware of His protection and encouragement. There is hope.

And maybe that's why I like to talk about the weather, because it seems like the sky suggests the coming of a better day. The morning is the epitome of hope. Dark night is over and the sky becomes brighter, and as on this morning, what seemed like a potentially threatening storm passed. And now a peaceful, cheerful morning is commencing.

We can look at that as the stages of devotional service that are dawning with our chanting. Every morning we have this hope and this opportunity, and even if we seem to blow it, to miss the chance, Kṛṣṇa gives us another chance with each dawn. But please Kṛṣṇa, help us so that we can actually make some permanent progress. That was my first question to Śrīla Prabhupāda: "Is there a level of spiritual advancement you can make from which one doesn't fall back?" Prabhupāda said yes. And I'm praying for that "yes" in my own *japa*. That means I still haven't achieved it, because every day I get sucked into that whirlpool of inattention *(durdaivam īdṛśam ihājani nānurāgaḥ).*

Sometimes devotees raise the question whether it's better to stop chanting rather than to go on chanting offensively. The answer is: Don't stop, keep walking down that road saying your *japa.* It's disappointing to know that your chanting is just a thin layer on top of your other cogitations, and you seem to be helpless to do anything about it. It's that feeling of failure and inability to change which produces frustration. So in the face of this, a person wants relief and stops chanting. But to stop chanting because we don't want to offend is just a rationalization. In actuality we've stopped out of frustration and inability to control the mind. Chanting inattentively is not pleasurable and we understand it's not pleasing to Kṛṣṇa, certainly not as pleasing as pure chanting, pure service. Bhaktivinoda Ṭhākura goes so far as to say inattentive chanting is not really chanting, but only a mouthing of the outer letters. We're aware of these things and that also makes us weary to keep uttering our "bad" mantras.

Let's take the beads out and keep putting what seems to us a thin layer of chanting on top of our earthly existence, because actually it's not an insignificant layer. It's a gesture by a weak person to Kṛṣṇa, the Almighty, and sooner or later Kṛṣṇa is going to be moved to give us some strength, some *bala,* so that we can actually serve the holy names.

July 13
Wicklow

Dear friends,

When I went out this morning it was darker than usual and raining. Far ahead on the road I saw an animal, probably a hare, who kept running forward instead of going into the underbrush at the side of the road. My mind was absorbed for awhile in looking at him. At the end of the road was the schoolhouse with a light coming from inside and beyond that, where I usually see the hills, there was only mist. I guess that explains why it's so dark. As for the light in the schoolhouse, Prabhupāda dāsa is there. Back from his weekend of book distribution and preaching to the Sunday guests in Dublin, he stayed overnight in the school. He's chanting his rounds now and will greet his four students when they come at 9:00 A.M.

Dear friends, our days are busy and we're in different parts of the world. I can't claim that I'm always thinking of you, but I think of you as I write these letters and I hope I can put something into them that will be true. I was about to say that I hope to write something worthwhile, by which I guess I meant instructive. That may be presumptuous of me—as if I place myself as your spiritual master and you as my disciples. The Vaiṣṇava scriptures tell us that one should not think like that—that I'm superior and have people serving me or that people are waiting to receive instruction from me. One should think of oneself as lower than the straw in the street.

It's nicer to think of you more as friends who want to hear spiritual knowledge and who are willing for me to reveal my mind, even my imperfections and doubts. Between friends there is no castigation or judgment, just exchanges. One friend says, I'm thinking like this or I'm feeling like this and the other listens sensitively, maybe makes suggestions. But mostly the friend hears and cares.

So I think of our letters like that, as based on a mutual interest in Kṛṣṇa conscious topics. But to reach topics we have to begin honestly by saying how we are doing in our practices.

I've been writing to you about chanting and I guess I don't have anything new to say, at least not in terms of my own progress. But it's always comforting to read about the glories of the holy name and figuratively "paste" the instructions in our notebook to remind us. For instance, it is good to remember that it is an offense to consider the glories of the holy name to be an exaggeration. Such a reminder can encourage one to worship the holy names, confident that to do so is the topmost *dharma*. Chanting Hare Kṛṣṇa is the easy-to-take, compact practice given by Lord Caitanya as the proper method of worship for this age.

Kṛṣṇadāsa Kavirāja Gosvāmī has recommended that we take one verse about chanting and string it like a garland around our necks. To emphasize this, he says that he is raising his arms and loudly proclaiming that we should please wear this garland around our necks when we're chanting and at all times. Just as the *kunti-mala,* or neckbeads, have become part of our lives, inseparable from our bodies, so in a similar way we should wear an invisible garland verse. Take for instance the second *Śikṣāṣṭakam* verse in which Lord Caitanya takes the role of a conditioned soul and laments that He chants without taste. In another *Śikṣāṣṭakam* verse Lord Caitanya starts to feel very humble about His lack of taste for chanting and about His position, thinking that there is nobody more fallen than Himself, not even the grass or the trees. In fact, these living entities have so many good qualities that He aspires to be like them, to have the tolerance of the tree, the humility of the grass.

Even now my acceptance of this verse is theoretical, but in the beginning it was hard to accept even on a theoretical basis. Such an extreme humility seemed too demanding of a devotee. Chanting is supposed to be easy, but such humility is impossible. Gradually we come to understand it's not something we can do on our own; it comes by mercy. But it is a fact that Lord Caitanya is being straightforward: this is required. If you want to chant constantly, which means if you want to chant with *ruci,* with *rāga,* this humility must come.

I can think of chanting steadfastly for so many years without gaining a higher taste, without even chanting with much attention. That's humbling in itself. It's also humbling to put our speculation aside and fully accept, with faith, that the holy names are Kṛṣṇa Himself.

As Prabhupāda used to say, "First deserve, then desire." We really have not been unfairly delayed in tasting the nectar of the holy names. Kṛṣṇa hasn't forgotten us. Nor have the holy names' powers been exaggerated. So we have to go on chanting, always taking the chanting period of our day as important and giving the chanting a good chance by providing the right atmosphere. And then, if everyday despite our trying to make good arrangements we are still inattentive, that's unfortunate. We still have to continue giving it the best time. We should not think this time could be spent more profitably doing something else. We should keep giving the chanting our best attention. And while we may humbly consider our chanting inferior, the fact is, we know it has at least some standing in our lives because we personally give it importance.

I told you I wasn't going to dwell on my silly distractions as if to secretly joke with you about poor chanting, (or to indulge in my memories). I just wanted to get it out on paper for my own sake and mention that this morning, I had some good things going for me. I was playing the tape of Prabhupāda chanting to keep me from drowsiness and inattention, and I was up early in the quiet morning. I have made so many arrangements to come to this retreat for chanting and reading, I have everything going for me, but still, my mind goes over such foolish things. That happens. Therefore, it's nice to have friends like you to whom I can reveal my mind. I hope sharing our experiences will lead to our mutually improved chanting.

I think I've told you that on morning walks, it's my habit to chant two rounds. Usually I don't think highly of taking *japa* walks, especially when devotees go out together. Nine times out of ten the walk turns into talk, not *japa*. Those talks are often important, but the *japa* has to have it's own time, so chanting and walking alone can be better. It's probably not recommended by most experts because the bodily movements and the variety of scenery tend to capture a person's attention and imaginations, and therefore his *japa* becomes only an accompaniment to those activities. But for me, the *japa* walk is a solace and it's often an improvement over the *japa* I chant indoors. Even with the best arrangements in the indoor *bhajana-kuṭir* you can become sleepy or inattentive. So, rather than fall into a torpor, you can go outdoors and get some fresh air. If you're in a lonely place like Wicklow, you can chant aloud to your heart's content. In the past, saints and Lord Caitanya Himself sang and chanted as they walked. Lord Caitanya used to walk and count His *japa* singing Kṛṣṇa Kṛṣṇa Kṛṣṇa. I agree that *japa* should be done sitting upright, but if you can't do that, try taking a walk with the Hare Kṛṣṇa mantra as your close companion.

To be honest, I have to add here that I'm feeling helpless. Although my letter today is somewhat instructive and upbeat, I don't want you to get the impression that I'm chanting nicely. Rather, as I was returning to the cottage, I saw that I have fallen into the pit of inattention. I was reminiscing that I was a high school student again riding home on the bus after a dance. I didn't have a date. On the same bus was one the most popular boys, Ned Finley, and with him was his date, Erma Fritsch, one of the most popular girls. So I relived a moment when the bus stopped. As I got off, Ned and his date said a few words to me. I imagined that they were condescending and joking and I was trying to appear chipper, but I was embarrassed by my lonely situation. When I caught myself in this imaginative reverie—and I was actually vocalizing the mantras while all this reminiscence was going on—I had a sensation of being physically very low. I suppose the weather added to that feeling, by the fact that the sky was overcast and I could only see the bottom of things. So there I was on the bottom, supposedly chanting Hare Kṛṣṇa. And supposedly writing this instructive letter, as if I know something you don't, as if I can tell you how to chant. So now, I'm asking you to please tell me, how can I control my mind? How can I simply be more attentive and more strict and not think that it's all right to remember and remember? Why should I think it's all right to forget what I'm actually doing?

July 14
Wicklow

Dear friends,

It's a nice day. Birds are chirping. I can see pink in the east through the window. The clouds are not so heavy. Some pale blue sky is showing for a change. Cool summer morning, begun by the routine of *bhajana.* And now has come my chance to talk to dear friends. We are serious people and like to talk about chanting and devotional service.

But is there any harm if we are startled and pleased to see an Irish green field just before sunrise? There's nothing wrong with rejoicing in God's nature, as long as we don't forget Him. Prabhupāda even said the ideal combination is a temple of Kṛṣṇa set within beautiful natural scenery. Similarly, if we walk through charming countryside, why shouldn't we be Kṛṣṇa conscious? In fact, that walk should be an impetus to Kṛṣṇa consciousness—just to see how glorious things are and how happy we become amid nature's beauties. As expressed by the poet Gerard Manley Hopkins, the "world is charged with the grandeur of God."

I want to talk about offenses in chanting and the nature of pure, unmotivated service. I thought of these things during an afternoon reading of *Śikṣāṣṭakam,* particularly verse four, *na dhanaṁ na janaṁ* . . . Did you know that in this verse, the word *kavitāṁ* specifically refers to beautiful poetry? Prabhupāda translates *sundarīṁ* as beautiful women. Literally speaking, Lord Caitanya says, "I don't want beautiful women and I don't want to enjoy beautiful poetry." This of course refers to poetry devoid of Kṛṣṇa consciousness. But the word *kavi* is not a bad word since there are such great *kavis* like Kavi Karṇapur and Rūpa Gosvāmī. In fact, one of the twenty-six qualities of a devotee is to be poetic. But Lord Caitanya doesn't want the poetry of this world just for its opulence in grammar and rhetoric or high thoughts or sensual impressions. The real essence of the *Śikṣāṣṭakam* verse is that devotional service should be performed without any desire except to please Kṛṣṇa. It's a very high standard, certainly. And that's Lord Caitanya's prayer. It may be above our heads because we still have motivations, but it's good to know the goal and to try to remove obvious motives in our Kṛṣṇa conscious practices.

Chanting too has to be pure and without motive. Mostly I've been writing to you about inattention, but that's just one of the ten offenses. Others are equally important, although they don't seem to be a direct part of the chanting *yajña*. Still, they're very much connected. For example, *sādhu-nindā*, or offense to the devotees. Not even chanting can clear offenses to devotees. You have to go to the devotee in one way or another and ask forgiveness.

I recently received a typed form letter from one of my Godbrothers. The salutation was typed Dear ________ and he had written my name in pen in the blank. He must have sent this letter out to a number of Godbrothers. It explained briefly that recently he had been criticizing me, thinking and sometimes speaking offensively about me. And therefore he wanted to admit this fault and ask forgiveness and resolve not to do it again. I thought the sentiment was nice and I'm sure he was sincere. I was a little amused that it was a form letter, which made it less personal, but he had exposed himself to many people at the same time. It was courageous.

But what do we do if we again commit the same offense? Do we send the form letter again? Still, it was an exemplary attempt, following the path of the *ācāryas* in how to deal with *sādhu-nindā.* I may be amused, but he's done better than I have. In fact, I took the opportunity to write him back and admit I've made offenses to him but that I should not do so because he is actually a very wonderful devotee. Anyway, we have to look for chances to reciprocate nicely with devotees whom we have sometimes unnecessarily criticized. This offense could be the reason we don't develop *bhāva* and *prema* even though we continue to chant. There must be a reason. This is certainly one possibility.

The countryside here is an artist's dream. There are many hills. Sometimes two hills will form a sharp valley and water will run down the gorge between the two hills. And then behind that conjunction of hills, another hill farther back will mount upward. This morning, the sky above the farthest hill was the color of the interior of an oyster. Some pink, some very light blue, and then a few milky clouds. That's a clear morning in Ireland. In the foreground were some hand-piled rock walls. The land in all directions was green. As I walked on the road, little balls of fur turned into moving hares ahead. By conveying these images, I'm writing you a postcard in the mood of "wish you were here," and I'm actually trying to wish you here by telling you what it's like.

It was quiet on the road, just the squeak-squeak of my rubber raincoat as my arms swung back and forth and the clop-clop of my rubber Wellington boots. By noticing these sounds I was able to glimpse the false ego in this body. He makes his own squeak-squeak, clop-clop, and yet I am not him.

Down the hill he comes. Squeak-squeak, clop-clop. Think-think, blink-blink. What does he see? A narrow road, once covered with tar and now cracking. A border of evergreens which stand shoulder-to-shoulder like guards. Is this person in the Wellington boots just a mechanical man? A wind-up toy? Those who say karma is everything might say we're forced to walk out the door, forced to write some attempt at poetry and letters, and, because the body is limited, forced to think of breakfast or discomfort. Everything in a karmic chain. But also there's some free will, although rare—especially the will to love Kṛṣṇa, which comes by Kṛṣṇa's grace. The conclusion is that I don't know anything. I don't know to what degree I'm a wind-up machine and to what degree I'm acting freely. But I pray, Lord, whether by rote, by force, or by free will, please engage me. Help me, guide me. Please protect my vows. Please let me love and let me show my love in acts for You. All glories to Prabhupāda.

July 15
Wicklow

Dear friends,

This morning the clouds were so low they came right down to the trees. It's the darkest morning yet. The summer isn't going to last forever. Gradually the sun will rise later and later.

In the darkness the lighted schoolhouse was bright and yellow. I knew that Prabhupāda dāsa was there chanting his *japa,* and I thought he might see me as I passed by.

It's nice to have everything in its place, to walk at the same time everyday, to be part of Kṛṣṇa's universe, where under His control, birds sing and evergreens whisper. Nothing is topsy-turvy, although it can become so if Kṛṣṇa gives the nod to Lord Śiva to begin his dance of destruction. But we hanker for the peaceful maintenance of the Lord. Within that maintenance, Kṛṣṇa gives us a certain life-duration and a quota of sense enjoyment, and we fill our life with *rajo-guṇa* activities. We *jīvas* basically waste our time trying to establish ourselves permanently in a temporary place. That's the civilization we live in. Hare Kṛṣṇa Hare Kṛṣṇa, Kṛṣṇa Kṛṣṇa Hare Hare/Hare Rāma Hare Rāma, Rāma Rāma Hare Hare. But Prabhupāda has come on Lord Caitanya's order to tell us that this world is false, that by chanting Hare Kṛṣṇa we can realize the real.

When things are going well (as they are for me nowadays, staying for a while in Ireland and taking morning walks), we sometimes ask ourselves, "How long will this last?" It's like a wish that the pleasant times should continue. I can see on the calendar just how long it will last, no more than twenty days. We ask the same question when we're in distress, "How long will this last?" In either case, the answer is that very soon it will end. And very soon we will meet the same fate which every living being has met who ever came into this world. Our time will be up. As we have a date of birth, likewise we have a date of death. For the time being, the date is unknown to us. In the Library of Congress data in the beginning of a book I've published, I see my name and date of birth, 1939, followed by a dash. The dash is an indication of a bit of clerical data that will be filled in shortly. One almost gets the impression that the Library of Congress computer is impatient for this information so that its file will be complete.

But our spiritual master has made these meditations more than dry humor. He has broken through the wall of death and pointed us to the next life. And now we live with that assurance. We're going to survive in one form or another. We can see death as a change, but not The End.

My morning walks begin in darkness and end at the time when the junction between land and sky is just beginning to lighten. On a foggy day like today, it is considerably lighter by the time I get back. This was a pleasing change. But I was reluctant to give up the privacy and protection of that brief time before the sun rises. That time is special, but like everything else, my attachment to its specialness has to be given up. Every day is an exercise in our letting go.

A special moment this morning: I was standing on the bridge and looking down into the water. The rapids were rushing over the rocks. The sound filled my ears and my whole body, that special hypnotizing sound of a creek when the air all around resonates with the rush of water. What can we say about such moments, especially when they are experienced just at dawn? But part of their beauty is that they have to be given up.

In the *Bhagavad-gītā* Kṛṣṇa says that the demons are attached to that which is temporary. They don't want to let the moment go. They want to consume it. And some atheists resign themselves to the temporary and even worship the fact that the heart feels poignant over its temporary nature. One knows that love will end, but still one goes ahead and loves anyway. For atheists and existentialists, real human responsibility is to make one's own reality and love it, even though one knows it ultimately has no meaning and is absurd. It's a crazy kind of philosophy. The existentialist says, I shall destroy everything, I shall deny God. "I shall blaspheme God and abandon my chance to worship Him, but still I'll try to be a good man, and this will be very brave of me. And for this, people will appreciate me, now and into posterity." This is nonsense—and very dangerous.

All glories to Lord Caitanya's *saṅkīrtana* and to His philosopher-followers. And thanks to my spiritual master, at whose lotus feet I bow.

Dawn brought pearl grays and dark greens, not the bright colors of a clear day. The subdued colors seemed to have their own smell—of smoke and animal dung and earth. Forgive me for rambling on. I really do like to talk about Kṛṣṇa and Kṛṣṇa's holy name with you, but I have an equally strong desire to put myself in this time and place, as if I could place myself in a box and wrap it up and put stamps on it and send it to you to say, "Here I am. Here's the way it was. Let's share."

Toward the end of the walk, it began to sprinkle and then rain lightly. My glasses fogged over, so I took them off and walked down a wet blurry road, chanting my two rounds. I am not qualified to think of Kṛṣṇa's pastimes in any developed way while chanting His names, but at least I can have faith and remember Prabhupāda's instruction to just hear the holy name. Prabhupāda taught this out of his own faith, that the absolute *cintāmaṇi* quality of the names will free us if we just hear them.

I chanted. The usual stuff came up, but I let it go. The pictures appeared in outline form, like in a coloring book, but I didn't take out my crayons and imaginatively color them in. I saw faces of boys and girls from my youth, remembered sitting on the swiveling tops of cafeteria stools and soda shop stools and bar stools, but I just let it go. Hare Kṛṣṇa Hare Kṛṣṇa, Kṛṣṇa Kṛṣṇa Hare Hare/ Hare Rāma Hare Rāma, Rāma Rāma Hare Hare.

In the countryside on a gray day, there's always a sense of freshness and of the earth's being replenished and so many creatures being sustained and the human spirit being refreshed and revived. Wet weather is fecund. I only wish that my spiritual life could feel similar rejuvenation.

July 16
Wicklow

Dear friends,

A new morning, a new letter. I was looking at some notes I kept for this letter and one note said, "Speak freely, knowing that you're with friends." There was also something about confessions. Confessions one makes to a friend are different from those one might make to a priest. In the Catholic Church the priest, as a representative of God, absolves one of sins. In our Gauḍīya Vaiṣṇava line, I don't think we regularly approach the guru to confess our sins and be absolved. Between friends, confession is more in the name of openness, honesty, and sharing. If we're to have a friendship and help each other in Kṛṣṇa consciousness, we shouldn't hide things. It's with that in mind that we confess to one another.

Having said that, I won't unburden myself now, but I hope that in the course of writing, when something comes up, I won't be afraid to say it.

I'm not bored with the countryside or the walk or my little weather report, if you're not bored hearing them. Today the clouds and the fog are so close that there is no sense of distance. In the dim light the simple rough cottages along the road moved in and out of the fog like apparitions. My heart felt happy, glad to be able to walk, by God's grace; but it was not that almost mystical pantheism at seeing the sunshine and the distances. Like the weather, I felt more closed in, quiet, so I walked and prayed to Kṛṣṇa, who is in our hearts as Supersoul.

In this mood I want to share with you, but my stores are so sparse that what can I share? At least I can tell you I'm still writing, still groping, never quite sure of the results. I'll give you a hint and say that I'm writing about Vṛndāvana-*bhajana* and whether it can be practiced in the West. That's the project I come away from when I go on the walk and when I return to write my letter to you.

I'm on a kind of retreat and am not seeing people, but I'm opening and receiving the mail. I'll be getting mail probably in a few days, in a package that has been forwarded to me. Maybe there will be something from you, which would be nice.

It's worth trying to say something more about chanting. It's like a daily communion between us, our talks about chanting. I think if it is done sincerely, one can never finish talking about *japa*, because the whole idea is to make chanting conscious, to take it out of the mechanical and unconscious. Just as I do not tire of telling you the daily weather report, I never tire of our *japa* talks.

I keep a votive candle lighted during my early morning *bhajana*. One votive candle I have is blue, so this morning, the blue light was flickering. But still, it wasn't going out. The idea of the light enduring and not going out despite it's flickering nature was, I felt, akin to the *japa*. We should have some assurance that we do have a light within us that wants to chant Hare Kṛṣṇa. That light is the spirit soul. And we should just keep bringing the mind back to the chanting itself, not worrying that the chanting is weak and might flicker and go out. Let's keep going.

I read something yesterday about the importance of eagerness, *utkāṇṭha,* in all spiritual activities. Without eagerness we cannot accomplish anything, even in the material world. And in spiritual activities, Kṛṣṇa reciprocates when He sees that we're keen to improve. A persistent eagerness or even anxiety to better our chanting will please Kṛṣṇa and cause Him to respond. We have to eagerly continue, not just make a little effort and then stop. In fact, our *dharma* is to practice. A perfect devotee is called *siddha,* meaning his nature is to chant Hare Kṛṣṇa. We should chant out of duty and never slacken that duty. That's all we have. At this stage in our devotional lives, duty is our expression of love. Therefore, determination is essential. I remember that Saint Teresa of Avila, speaking in her native language, said that spiritual life had to be practiced with "mui determinado determinacion," with a very determined determination. So that's *vaidhī-bhakti.* That's where we're at. And if we put a lot into our practice, duty will start to turn into devotion.

Kṛṣṇa will respond according to how we approach Him. If we approach Him through the *mahā-mantra,* Kṛṣṇa will become interested in our chanting. He will touch it. Therefore, let every day find us up early, making the best arrangement to chant the Hare Kṛṣṇa mantra. If inattention seems inevitable, we should not be deterred from making the "impossible" attempt. For the time being, if I can think of the holy name just a little bit, that will be a gain. If I can at least be awake and speak the mantras with occasional focus, that will be my beginning. And from there I can try to go further.

We shouldn't practice all alone, and therefore it's good to share with one another how we are progressing. And if we get that rare opportunity to be with devotees who chant well, we can inquire from them how to improve. Sometimes their answers may not be very startling or unusual. They may respond with something you've read in scripture or heard other sages say. However, just hearing from advanced devotees—if we hear with faith—can lead to a breakthrough. Prabhupāda's repeated advice about chanting was to hear the holy name, so we can meditate on that concise instruction and actually try to follow it.

A passage I read yesterday in the *Nectar of Devotion* offered encouragement about the importance of chanting. It was in the chapter describing the characteristics of steady ecstasy, such as not wasting time, and always expecting the mercy of Kṛṣṇa. One of those qualities is *ruci, nāma-sadā-ruci,* which means having a taste for chanting the Lord's holy names.

Rūpa Gosvāmī gives an example, a statement about Rādhārāṇī to the effect that this girl (and we know it's Rādhārāṇī) has eyes filled with tears and She is always chanting Kṛṣṇa's name. This is more evidence that chanting is not just for the *sādhaka*. Even in Vraja there is pure chanting of Kṛṣṇa's name, and when they chant, all ecstasies come. Lord Caitanya prayed for the day when that kind of chanting would come, when tears would flow from His eyes.

You may be thinking, "But what is *japa* actually like for you?" During any particular round, I really don't seem to be able to hear the holy names at all. I notice them at the end of the round because then I have a small sense of satisfaction as I reach the counter bead. Sometimes my mind listens to the chanting for a while, but it's never with a holy passion. If I had to point out something positive about my own *japa* it would be an underlying tenacity to always continue chanting, which in itself borders on a kind of spiritual passion. Usually a person can only be convinced of something if he has some experience of its good result. For myself, even without experience of any advanced symptoms, I am convinced that I will always chant and always consider it very important and tell others about its importance. In a sense, what I feel while chanting is irrelevant. I know that I don't experience ecstasy, but so what? Even without any sign of hope for improvement, I'm convinced of the importance of chanting in my life. It links me to Śrīla Prabhupāda. So there, I've confessed that I have an attachment to the holy name of Kṛṣṇa.

While I was finishing my walk this morning, as I was coming back down the hill toward the cottage, I saw a person a few hundred yards past the cottage. It was Madhu. He was well camouflaged in his drab green coat, but I clearly saw his bright orange bead bag. He remained at a distance chanting and looking down into the water from the bridge. When I saw him I thought, "I bet Madhu is praying as he chants." I know from discussions I have had with him that as he chants, he tries to pray to Rādhā and Kṛṣṇa. To have an inclination for that is good. When I was just boasting to you about my attachment to the holy name, I didn't mention praying because it's not so much in my program, but here I saw Madhu and thought of it. Therefore I wanted to mention it to you, and to myself: let's try to pray as we chant.

July 17
Wicklow

Dear friends,

I relish our exchanges—sharing Kṛṣṇa consciousness with friends, reading letters back and forth, sharing time together, going together as fellow students to see the spiritual master and the grand-spiritual master, riding together in cars and planes and rickshaws, and while doing these things, talking about the activities in eternal Vraja-*dhāma* as well as immediate concerns, like who's going to pay for the taxi. Sometimes we share bodily complaints, sometimes we sit together to take *prasādam,* but always we consider how to avoid offenses to other devotees, try to curb each other's tendencies to cause offense and we hear each other out. Friends share in Kṛṣṇa consciousness.

Last year a friend suggested that I teach a seminar on the life of Prabhupāda. So I'm doing it. Maybe I gave him a book to help him in his writing. Devotees try to exchange in this way, writing notes even when we're living in the same place, laughing together.

So my friends, what will we talk about this morning? I feel like you're present and waiting to hear from me. I don't want to disappoint you. Just by your being willing and present, I'm able to say things I couldn't say otherwise.

Yesterday we continued reading *Śikṣāṣṭakam* and got to the seventh verse. As you know, the *ācāryas* say the seventh and eighth verses are

Lord Caitanya expressing himself in the mood of Śrīmatī Rādhārāṇī. In some of the previous verses He expresses Himself as a practicing devotee. But then He says that He feels the world void without the presence of Kṛṣṇa. It may seem so far from our stage of devotion as to not be applicable to us. The feeling of lacking love for Kṛṣṇa is the ultimate stage. But actually it is helpful to hear Lord Caitanya saying in the mood of Rādhārāṇī, *govinda-viraheṇa me.* Even at the beginning stage, we need to feel that inadequacy in our life. We are not satisfied just by gathering material amenities. What's missing? Our love for Kṛṣṇa, *govinda-viraheṇa me.*

We shouldn't think this is impractical talk. Even if we persist with what we consider to be practical devotional service—amassing heaps of quantifiable results in terms of money collected or books distributed or books written or *japa* chanted—if it's missing the affection for Kṛṣṇa, it hasn't yet come to the proper stage. We could go on and on amassing and amassing so-called practical service and still not reach *prayojana.*

It's one of the truly inconceivable things about spiritual life how the pure devotee feels unhappy because of Kṛṣṇa's absence. I say inconceivable because we have such a firmly rooted idea that unhappiness is undesirable and one of the reasons we look for spiritual life is to become happy. We don't want these material miseries. Spiritual life promises joy. Therefore, why do Gauḍīya Vaiṣṇavas say when you get to the highest stage, you're miserable again? It's not easy to understand, but the pure devotees in Vraja do seem to be quite unhappy externally, crying without end and becoming thin when it appears that Kṛṣṇa has deserted them. Such things are beyond our current understanding. That's all we can say for now. However, with faith and by hearing from the *ācāryas*, we accept that it is not a material unhappiness. This pain of separation is a way of being with Kṛṣṇa.

Being close to Kṛṣṇa and serving Him is the essence of Kṛṣṇa consciousness. So when Kṛṣṇa is away, the perfect devotee misses Him, thinks of Him, and remembers His pastimes, until Kṛṣṇa is present again. We call it separation, but actually it's not. The world may seem void because Kṛṣṇa does not appear in the world to the external vision, but a devotee sees Kṛṣṇa within. Pure devotees love Kṛṣṇa so much that they could not go on living unless they thought of Him. Their thoughts of Kṛṣṇa are all they live for. Everything else has been abandoned. The world with all its opulence and variety appears void. Even the variety of Irish mornings would have no meaning. Food has no meaning. Sleep has no meaning. And that is why Raghunātha dāsa Gosvāmī practices austerities, not to curb the senses, but rather, because when Kṛṣṇa is absent, Raghunātha has no taste for, or attachment to, material functions.

We can get a small sense of this when we sometimes become so absorbed in our Kṛṣṇa conscious activities that we neglect material functions to some degree. We needn't worry about neglecting our health. Our minds are so focused on survival that they will take care of those responsibilities. But if we do start to lose interest and see the world as not having any opportunities, that's a good thing, because then we can shift our energy to Kṛṣṇa.

I've probably said enough about this for now. I'm just speaking what I've read and it's over my head, but I've shared it with you this morning because I thought it was most important. Therefore, it's nice to have a friend who's willing to hear one day about *viraha* and another day about rabbits on the road.

This morning after walking for half an hour, I turned to start back in the other direction. Almost as an afterthought I noticed the moon. In fact, I half-noticed it, turned away, then looked back at the moon again. We're just tiny creatures and the moon is a huge planet, but the way we're situated we can give the moon our attention or not. This morning the sky was blue, and by 5:30 it was getting light. So the moon was about to disappear. It was full of pock marks, white and delicate and off in the distance. Unlike the flickering of my *japa,* the moon is steady. I think of the story Prabhupāda told in a lecture in 1966 at 26 Second Avenue. In his youth, as a *gṛhastha,* he was walking with his youngest son. His son looked up and said, "Father, why is the moon following us?" Prabhupāda then said that as the moon always goes with us on the street, God is always with us when we chant Hare Kṛṣṇa. Prabhupāda didn't explain it further. We are so tiny and the moon is so far away, but still the moon goes with us. God is so great. He seems so far away on His spiritual planet, but by the appearance of the Lord in the holy name, He can go with us while we walk.

I may have noticed the moon only as an afterthought today, but chanting shouldn't be like that. We should notice the beauty and mercy of Kṛṣṇa's holy name right from the start. But in case we forget, He remains there, brilliant, inviting. He is not going away with the dawn. When we do turn to Him, we can have the full embrace of Kṛṣṇa's holy name. We should feel sorry that we've left such a brilliant friend, such a warm, beautiful companion as *kṛṣṇa-nāma.* The real test of whether we have some genuine regret is if we resolve not to again stray from our friend and whether we make efforts to chant in earnest. It can be done. Hare Kṛṣṇa.

July 18
Wicklow

Dear friends,

Usually when I talk about my walks I tell you about what I see, what it's like out there, and about what the real charm of the walks is for me, what I experience. But walking itself is a great joy. Too often we take it for granted that we can walk. It's a God-given ability. Prabhupāda commented how nowadays people don't walk very much. He would say, "They will move not one inch on leg, but everything has to be done by car." In former days to go from Bengal to Vṛndāvana, or to cover all of South India or North India, people would travel on foot. And that's what *pada-yātrā* is, and *parikrama.* I'm not always able to be in the holy *dhāmas* for *parikramas,* and even when I am there I can't keep up with the pace of others. But to take my little morning *parikrama* and see a robin sitting on a post and then flittering away, to see a dark sky with just a little light in the east—this is bliss, because I see Kṛṣṇa behind it.

One of the remarkable things that I notice about Irish weather is how quickly it changes, especially the sky. Like this morning, as I started out there were very heavy clouds, but considerable patches were clear. In the east, through a hole in the clouds, shone a bright, dramatic dawn, almost like the opening notes of a symphony. But by the time I noted it, it was practically gone. This morning the east was gray and troubled, but the north was a clear light blue with streaks of clouds. Just as in the world there will be war in one country, but across the ocean, there will be apparent peace.

I have to say, I never had such a sensation that clouds could come down to earth. You think of clouds usually as way up there, but here, clouds come right down to the low hills and even into the valleys. You may say that's fog or mist rising from the ground, but it looks as if the same big, fluffy wet things that float in the sky have come right down to the earth and are rolling over it.

I noticed big puddles on the road. Then I remembered there had been heavy rainfall during the night. I remember waking up around 11:30 and hearing it pounding. I got up and closed the skylight. Anyway, that accounts for the puddles and the fact that the stream under the bridge is louder than usual and more forceful. The tar-topped road looked soaked through. It isn't one of those ultra-modern jobs, this road. You can see pebbles mixed with the black tar. Although the water really doesn't soak through it, the road this morning has the appearance of a soaked object. The puddles were full of sky, like mirrors. They were brighter than the air around.

What is it that makes us so cheerful to see a sparrow-sized bird sitting on a bush? There's really not that much fellowship between us and our "feathered friends," but they speak to the human being's desire to be happy and full of song when we see them in the morning. Where does that joy come from? From a Kṛṣṇa conscious point of view, we know that behind every perverted reflection there is a reality. The joy has to come from somewhere, and that source is pure, spiritual joy. So it would certainly be the most unhappy conclusion to say that what appears to be joyful in this world is illusion. Kṛṣṇa consciousness teaches us about the *sanātana-dharma* from which everything comes. That knowledge enriches and enlightens our perception of this world. There are all kinds of birds, large and small, in Vraja-*dhāma*. Parrots come and tell Kṛṣṇa where Rādhā is and what is happening in different places in the forests. And by these messages, Kṛṣṇa is informed about what to do and where to go in order to taste the best nectar. In fact, Śukadeva Gosvāmī is one of those parrots.

I know I'm going too far when I start becoming absorbed in the here and now. I know this moment is going to end and to become absorbed in it leads in the wrong direction. But when I recall that God is behind what I see and touch and feel, then I can adjust. I don't say that I've mastered this. Rather I have a tendency to think it's wrong to appreciate nature, especially outside the holy places of India. And that feeling, according to our philosophy, is partly right, but it feels a little negative. We haven't completely adjusted yet to understand how God is behind nature. It is wrong to think of weeds and snakes and buttercups and dandelions and in so doing forget Kṛṣṇa, the Supreme Personality of Godhead. That would be a form of *māyā*, induced you might say by the enchanting fairies and leprechauns who cast *mahā-māyā* in all the delicate and powerful varieties we call nature. Nature is unsullied by man's interference, so it gives us relief. But to walk around and bathe our eyes in natural sights is a kind of sense gratification. We have to combine such relief with the actual relief of the soul. Prabhupāda talks about nature studies, so there's plenty that we can learn from nature, which is like a Kṛṣṇa conscious textbook. For instance, I came across a dead but perfectly formed frog. How he died I don't know. Although nature gave him a body that functions very well within its limitations, it's own *śakti,* still, death has come. In this way we can get lessons from nature.

July 19
Wicklow

Dear friends,

A new morning, but so rainy I had to carry an umbrella. The clouds, dark and full of rain, looked a little malevolent. Their dark forms shifted and pulled, but the clouds seemed to be tied to the top of the hill by smoke-like ropes.

Shall I tell you about our reading last night of *Śikṣāṣṭakam,* verse eight? It's an esoteric verse. Lord Caitanya is speaking in the mood of Śrīmatī Rādhārāṇī. When we think of it as coming directly from Rādhārāṇī, the verse becomes even more striking. In the last chapter of *Caitanya-caritāmṛta,* Lord Caitanya, through the words of Kṛṣṇadāsa Kavirāja, gives His own commentaries on His *Śikṣāṣṭakam* verses. And there it is clear that His verse was actually spoken by Śrīmatī Rādhārāṇī. And who is Lord Caitanya but Śrīmatī Rādhārāṇī combined with Kṛṣṇa?

I remember an incident involving this verse. In 1976 when Prabhupāda visited the Fifty-fifth Street temple in Manhattan, I came to see him there. I entered a room where he was speaking to many guests. Prabhupāda gestured that I should come forward. In the course of his conversation he mentioned this verse—"I do not know anyone but Kṛṣṇa as my Lord"—and surprised me by asking me to explain what it meant. I began saying what I had heard Prabhupāda say about the verse, how Rādhārāṇī will love Kṛṣṇa even if

He doesn't come before Her, even if He makes Her broken-hearted. Prabhupāda interrupted me and said, "There is no business exchange." I didn't take his interruption to mean I was wrong, but that he wanted to make the most concise and definitive statement. This verse shows that when we love Kṛṣṇa, we should do it without expecting something in return; otherwise, it's not love. Prahlāda Mahārāja said something similar when Lord Nṛsiṁhadeva offered him a boon. Prahlāda replied, "My Lord, please don't ask me to request a reward for my service. I'm not a businessman. It's my duty to serve You in love."

Again this is the question of rendering service without motivation. I offer these thoughts so we might deliberate how we can serve in this way.

Prabhupāda so mercifully taught us this and engaged us in this mood from the very beginning of our training. He pushed us into selfless service by his own example and by somehow creating this exciting movement, ISKCON. Remember how ISKCON blossomed in the early seventies? It attracted so many people who were the flower of youth of various countries, all of whom gratefully embraced Prabhupāda's lotus feet. And those devotees, boys and girls, went out and worked under austere conditions to create the Kṛṣṇa consciousness movement. It was done without expectation of reward. It was not a business that Prabhupāda set up, and that's what made it so attractive. We had had enough of business. But Prabhupāda said, "You come and work for Kṛṣṇa. There is no pay, but you can live in the temples and feel the bliss of serving the Lord and chanting His holy name."

Dear friend, I wish I could link this topic to what we've been talking about everyday: the chanting. I suppose I don't chant with a business mentality, expecting a return. But we expect more of ourselves, thinking that by now we should be able to fix our minds on Kṛṣṇa's name. As Śrīla Prabhupāda had to face disappointments with his boys and girls in the new movement when married couples broke up and so many devotees fell down and gave up their vows, so we're somewhat disappointed in ourselves, even if we continue to follow the principles. We're learning that it's not everything to stick to the rules and regulations. That in itself doesn't bring us the deep satisfactions and ecstasies described as symptoms of the *bhakti-mārga.* But I don't want to lament. At least we can take credit that we don't chant with the idea of a business return.

That's perhaps the saving grace of our chanting; we're not getting the reward of higher taste and still we chant. This means that the energy we're putting into it is devotional labor of a sort. So we can pray with an infinitesimal degree of the mood of Lord Caitanya's *Śikṣāṣṭakam,* "O holy name, O Lord Kṛṣṇa, O Śrīmatī Rādhārāṇī, even if You make me broken-hearted by not being present before me (due to my offenses), still, You are always my Lord unconditionally. You can do as You like, but I will never stop serving *hari-nāma.*"

Let me tell you what happened on my way back from the walk. I saw that some of the neighbor's cows had gotten out of their pasture. Some were on the road and some were standing around the devotees' little schoolhouse, like children waiting for school to open. Big, big bulls and cows with that doomed look on their faces, it seems to me. We don't see that expression on the faces of Kṛṣṇa's cows on our farms. By the time I met them, it was pouring rain, I just walked by chanting.

What's it like where you are?

July 21
Wicklow

Dear friends,

I didn't write yesterday because I was sick. I didn't go for a walk.

On today's walk the sky around the moon was a perfect blue. The moon was sliced in half and very bright. In the east I could see the bowl of the hill and its greenery, a sight which is sometimes obscured on a cloudy day. Over the hill Kṛṣṇa had smudged some blue clouds. He seemed to be working in a different medium—blue charcoals or watercolors.

And so, dear friends, these are my walks and my letters to you, part of my life and part of your life. I did get some mail, but didn't get a letter from you. That's all right. I know I will be getting one soon. And in the meantime our letters go out. They don't have to cross exactly one for one as long as I know that you're there, wanting to hear. And as long as we have Kṛṣṇa at the center. Kṛṣṇa, that intensely blue person whose lotus feet are the shelter for the whole world. That Kṛṣṇa who does not belong to this material world. But by the grace of the devotees and the grace of Kṛṣṇa's own *śāstra,* we know Him and His appearance. Indeed, Kṛṣṇa has revealed Himself fully in the literatures of the six Gosvāmīs. We understand Kṛṣṇa from the viewpoint of His beloved Śrīmatī Rādhārāṇī.

I was hearing a tape this morning of myself and other devotees reading the *Vidagdha-mādhava.*

Do you know that play by Rūpa Gosvāmī? *Vidagha-mādhava* is about *pūrva-rāga,* the sweetness of the first meeting between Rādhā and Kṛṣṇa? Even in this world, first love is the most exciting and beautiful. It transforms the lovers into almost mad persons. Of course, in the material world that first love inevitably fades. But because Rādhā and Kṛṣṇa are infinite and perfect, They always have *pūrva-rāga* and anticipation to meet, even later when they get to know each other. *Vidagdha-mādhava* tells how Rādhā as a young girl starts to dream about Kṛṣṇa. Then She hears His flute and becomes transformed in so many ways. She realizes that Her whole life has changed and that Her chastity and respectability are lost. But She loves Kṛṣṇa so much. To increase Her love for Kṛṣṇa, Her friends Paurṇamāsī, Lalitā, and Viśākhā draw a picture of Kṛṣṇa to show Her. Rādhārāṇī says, "My chastity is so lost that I'm now madly attracted to three persons: Kṛṣṇa who plays the flute, Kṛṣṇa who appears in My dreams, and now this person in the picture." Her friends tell Her, "Śrīmatī, these three persons are all aspects of the one person, Kṛṣṇa."

So I say, *Jaya Vidagdha-mādhava. Jaya* Śrīla Rūpa Gosvāmī. I'm becoming more interested in Kṛṣṇa's Vṛndāvana pastimes, as Prabhupāda requested of us, and I hope you are too. If I could hear more about this from you, we could start a dialogue. I'm hesitant because how we share Kṛṣṇa consciousness together is confidential. And because the subject matter is confidential we have to have some agreement about it.

It's a great challenge to us to read such literatures, because this is pure love between the young beautiful boy and the young beautiful girl. We are so contaminated with material desires. There may even be a tendency among devotees to shy away or remain uninterested in Kṛṣṇa and His pastimes in Vṛndāvana. This may be unhealthy. We've received many warning not to take *kṛṣṇa-līlā* cheaply, but that is so we may proceed in the right way. The warnings are not intended to bar us from Kṛṣṇa's pastimes.

As I say this I recall the sign: "Warning—Danger," which the army has posted to warn people not to enter their firing range. The sign warns not to go further. But that is not Prabhupāda's message. He tells us, go further, but do it properly.

More often than not it's a kind of worldliness which prevents us from further interest in Kṛṣṇa. Sometimes a devotee actually has some lack of faith in Kṛṣṇa. Getting too close to Kṛṣṇa's pastimes makes the devotee feel uneasy, because he may consider the pastimes to be myths. I'm speaking of a devotee who has officially committed himself to Kṛṣṇa consciousness, who enters public forums as a devotee and advocates *Bhagavad-gītā,* but is not able to go very deeply into the philosophy. Because he has a strong desire to serve he engages in duties, but tries not to think too deeply about Kṛṣṇa. He may take to Deity worship in the temple, seeing that the offerings are made on time, arranging for new outfits to be made, and making all arrangements for the Deity worship to continue. He may actually go before the temple Deities and pray with devotion. But to connect the pastimes of Kṛṣṇa with the Deities or with the chanting has not yet come to this devotee.

Why is that? I guess, as with anything, Kṛṣṇa has not yet graced the devotee with that realization. All advancement is due to two factors: the endeavor of the devotee and the grace of the Lord. We might suggest that when the grace does not appear, there may be some lack of endeavor also. Therefore let us endeavor in the right way to try to realize that Kṛṣṇa's pastimes are real, that Kṛṣṇa is actually a person. And I think the way to do that is to keep hearing more and more descriptions.

Sometimes a description of Kṛṣṇa will catch our imagination in such a way that for the first time, we realize Kṛṣṇa is not just the historical God, the Supreme Head, but is actually a person, just like we've always told others He is. I had a flash of this recently when I was hearing a description of Śrīmatī Rādhārāṇī in a poem by Rūpa Gosvāmī. I forget the exact situation. Somebody had said something to Rādhārāṇī as She was bowing down to Paurṇamāsī, who is actually *yoga-māyā*. And, as is often the case, Rādhārāṇī was concealing Her actual feelings of intense love for Kṛṣṇa. But She was bowing down in a very modest way and offering obeisances. I don't know, but just by hearing it, I suddenly appreciated that Rādhārāṇī was the goddess of Vṛndāvana. The more we can hear, the more chance there will be for doors to suddenly be opened for us—by the grace of the spiritual master.

July 22
Wicklow

Dear friends,

I'm glad to sit down to write you. I want to keep up this correspondence indefinitely. Hare Kṛṣṇa Hare Kṛṣṇa, Kṛṣṇa Kṛṣṇa Hare Hare/Hare Rāma Hare Rāma, Rāma Rāma Hare Hare. A clear day today. No raincoat. There was more blue sky than clouds on this morning's walk and within the clouds, fluffed throughout, was a faint rose color, barely perceptible among the blue and gray tints. I imagine the only reason I saw it today is because everything was so clear. Nature is a manifestation of Kṛṣṇa's energy; Kṛṣṇa Himself remains in the personal form that most interests us. He remains in Vraja. But because now we know about Kṛṣṇa, even when we look at nature we know whose energy it is. Depending on the intensity of our references to original Kṛṣṇa, anything may remind us of Him, even a cloud. But still, original Kṛṣṇa is different.

This morning I saw something I've never seen before on my walks here—three deer. Even from a distance they seemed to be aware of me. The largest extended his neck, raised his ears and nose, trying to catch any sound or smell of me as I thumped my way down the hill. They got wind of me at quite a distance and ran a little ways, then stopped again. Suddenly they leaped over a fence and out of harm's way. Their gracefulness called to mind descriptions of deer in Kṛṣṇa's Vṛndāvana pastimes. I thought of the *gopīs* speaking about the foolish deer who have seen Kṛṣṇa, but who will not tell the *gopīs* where He is, and the deer that go together in pairs to hear and appreciate the nectar of Kṛṣṇa's flute, the nectar of His smiling face, and the nectar of His beautiful body, which they lick. In this way, the wives of the deer are more fortunate than the *gopīs*, because the *gopīs'* husbands are not so appreciative of their wives' love for Kṛṣṇa.

What delight it is to see such sights and have them serve as reminders of Kṛṣṇa's pastimes. A morning walk accompanied by such thoughts lifts the heart. But a thoughtful person sometimes suspects his own cheerfulness. I remember reading that statement in Thoreau. He said he felt so happy that perhaps it was just animal spirits. But a devotee can dive into happiness in terms of appreciating Kṛṣṇa's greatness. That's his foundation, always. The happiness may enter the body and the mind from the nose or the mouth in the form of clear fresh air on a morning walk. The happiness may freshen his eyes as he sees the tasseled tops of weeds on the roadside dancing in the breeze. And he notices better the different shades of green and the way the fern leaves are shaped. Other leaves are reminiscent of childhood. Is that poison ivy? Is that blackberry? Is that wild strawberry? There are so many different weeds. In this way, happiness can invade the body and mind, but then he thinks of how Kṛṣṇa is so great. He's saved from turning down another blind alley when he realizes that everything is temporary and he's just been experiencing some euphoria.

By Kṛṣṇa's energy the material world is so beautiful, and the things that are most beautiful and that touch devotees most have a real semblance to the spiritual world. For example, I've told you about some of the points of the walk and how enchanting they are. One of them is the stream, which is always rapid because of all the rain. In some places it is not wider than ten feet across. Every inch of it ripples and trembles and moves forward. White foam collects around the rocks. Old rocks. And because the time is July, both sides of the stream are thick with grass, ferns, and weeds. The stream is tumbling down, down, down from the hills. This stream looks like streams we've seen in paintings depicting the pastimes of Kṛṣṇa in Vṛndāvana. So does the land. Cows are grazing. Kṛṣṇa is not here, we do not hear His flute, but the whole setting is here for meditation. Kṛṣṇa Kṛṣṇa Kṛṣṇa.

July 23
Wicklow

Dear friends,

Before I went out on my walk, while I still was chanting my rounds, it occurred to me that the things that are faulty in me are the same things I confront over and over. I seemed to see clearly what they were: these are my faults; this is what I have to overcome. The fact that we keep working at the same things makes it clear that we are limited and stunted in a particular way. It doesn't matter how hard we try, these defects remain. I suppose you could make an analogy to the physical body. If a person is missing a foot, there's no way to get another, although he can compensate for the loss. Defects in character, especially things that prevent us from spiritual advancement, are not permanent handicaps, although they may seem that way.

I needn't accept my faults as permanent. Before I was a devotee, I had characteristic habits and activities; now they're completely gone. I'm thinking particularly of things like sex and intoxication that are against the regulative principles. These activities have stopped. So there's cause for optimism. But neither should it be so terrible to look in the face of my favorite *"anarthas"* or character defects with hopes of overcoming them.

You have yours. I have mine. And part of friendship is not to hate each other for those defects, but to try to help each other work on them.

Take the Irish weather. Ireland is not going to become Bermuda. It has a different climate. But the rain and chill are not going to prevent a person who is determined to become Kṛṣṇa conscious. This morning it was completely dark—the darkest morning yet. No hills. The sky hanging close to the ground. At any moment it could rain. The farmer overcomes the weather in order to do his duty. In winter one still bathes and in the heat of summer a woman still cooks in the kitchen. So why shouldn't a devotee who lives in a particular land or in a particular body not be able to overcome his spiritual limitations and transcend? I mean to say these things as way of encouragement, but I don't want to overstress endeavor as if it can accomplish everything. I guess all these factors serve to put us in a condition of prayer at the lotus feet of guru and Kṛṣṇa: Please rescue me from my particular defect and limitation, please accept my service despite its impurity determined by place, culture, and the particular person I am by karma. I am sorry for these things I can't seem to overcome, and I pray that you please let me serve You in a way that's not so encumbered.

All the factors of culture and personality are so complex and overwhelming that we think of them as the total self, but we devotees realize that this is not the case. This big, sticky ball of material life is illusion, like a complicated dream. And we pray to Kṛṣṇa to please accept our chanting of the universal wake up call: Hare Kṛṣṇa—*jīv jāgo, jīv jāgo.* Let us wake up and glorify Kṛṣṇa. Kṛṣṇa will not mind if our prayers are offered in particular dialects or with personal idiosyncrasies. He will accept the essence.

The most wonderful human story is that of the soul rising above the conditioned state. It's a story that I like to tell. There are many ways we can tell it, through different characters and fictional pieces, or through our own story. And the attempt of individual devotees all over the world, in different places and situations, to rise above the conditioned state, is the real activity in the material world. When these devotees join together and assist the Kṛṣṇa consciousness movement under the direction of an empowered soul like Śrīla Prabhupāda, a spiritual force arises that can actually change the sorry state of this world. Prabhupāda has done so much work already; now the devotees are trying to carry it on.

Because we're speaking personally and intimately, I want to make a confession. I have a tendency to want to evoke my life of practicing devotional service. It could be seen as an obsession, but I'm trying to purify it. One form it takes is a desire to preserve life experience. One wants to live with some intensity, especially the intensity of appreciation for the precious gift of life however it comes. It is my desire to evoke the experiences of individuals perceiving the world, whether we speak of the atmosphere of sky or the struggle to change one's life, and to preserve these experiences in some form as art, I suppose. Art has at its center the desire to evoke and preserve, so that through art, experience may be shared by others in an act of communion. That communion between sensitive souls, the artist and the perceiver of art, is itself a most valuable and wondrous thing. But it falls dismally short if you leave Kṛṣṇa out of the picture. When Kṛṣṇa is in the center of this endeavor, it becomes something very important. It can encourage people to continue in their devotional service and invite those who are not yet practicing to begin.

The stories of how a devotee comes to Kṛṣṇa consciousness are among the favorite stories devotees share. A person coming to Kṛṣṇa consciousness may have overcome some oppressive situation such as opposition from parents or the government. At the beginning, circumstances may have been very difficult, but still, Kṛṣṇa guided the devotee on, sometimes touching the devotee's life in extraordinary ways. To hear these stories is encouraging.

Even the conversion stories of great souls like Nārada Muni or Vālmīki are among our favorites in the śāstric narrations. For when we hear how Śukadeva Gosvāmī or the Kumāras were impersonalists and became devotees, we see the potency of the spiritual energy and how it touches lives. And then we think, yes, it's real, it's true, and I can do it too. The example of others also impels us to want to make our own story a success, not an aborted tale of someone who came and then fell away.

The initial coming to Kṛṣṇa consciousness is a triumphant story. But it would be superficial to end all the stories by saying, "And then she moved into the temple and lived happily ever after in Vaikuṇṭha bliss." That initial story has many subsequent chapters. Those are harder to write.

Sometimes the story ends after a few chapters when someone quits practicing apparently for this lifetime. Or the story gets lost in so many duties and we only reminisce about the time that we rose up as a spirit soul. Or, as I said in the beginning of this letter, we keep hitting up against the wall of the same personal defects, the same limitations, and it seems like we can go no further. So in that case, rather than say "She lived happily ever after," we would say, "And then after twenty years, she realized she could go no further because she could never overcome her basic defects." That's not a very triumphant ending. Let's keep going and find a way to get Kṛṣṇa's mercy so that we can say and feel, *"Jaya Jaya* Śrī Kṛṣṇa—*paraṁ vijayate śrī-kṛṣṇa-saṅkīrtanam."*

One way to go about this is to realize we have to summon up the kind of courage we had in the beginning when we threw off so many ties and came to Kṛṣṇa consciousness. And we have to receive a burst of mercy, like we did in the beginning. We have to acknowledge that we haven't reached perfection, nor have we reached a dead end. We can go further. Hare Kṛṣṇa.

July 25
Wicklow

Dear friends,

I've become addicted to writing to you. I think it's a good thing. I know that I could just as well be silent and the world would be no different. But I have this urge to not let time go by without having tried to talk with you. It seems like an addition to my existence to say something, and that's because of the gift we have of Kṛṣṇa consciousness.

I hope that Kṛṣṇa will be pleased that we are speaking among ourselves, trying to help each other. Kṛṣṇa says in *Bhagavad-gītā* that He's pleased with His devotees who are characterized by their liking to enlighten one another. Therefore we have assurance from Kṛṣṇa.

But I want to make sure that Kṛṣṇa is the basis of my letter-writing; otherwise, it will be as insignificant as many love letters or business correspondence or notes between friends which, after the people die, are put in a trunk and forgotten.

Someone here asked me how we can remember Kṛṣṇa more. It seems to me that the more we hear about Kṛṣṇa's activities, the more we can naturally think of Him. If we don't hear about Kṛṣṇa's pastimes, we will tend to think of Him as that vague person, God—He who knows everything, He who hears our prayers, He who helps and protects us. Of course, these are eternal qualities of God and we may pray in a personal way to that omnipotent being, to that indwelling guide. This mystical prayer is common to many religions. At this mystical level we all pray to the same aspect of God and can develop a personal relationship with Him.

But there is something better than that in Kṛṣṇa consciousness. In Kṛṣṇa consciousness we become attracted to Kṛṣṇa, the original personal form of the Supreme Lord. In His personal form, Kṛṣṇa takes pleasure in His devotees. Prabhupāda gives the example of a judge who is not so much himself in court but who, at home, is relaxed and takes pleasure in being with his family. God as the indwelling guide, as a friend of the conditioned souls, He is not expressing Himself in terms of His own pleasure potency and delight when He's relating with pious people. But when somebody really wants to please Kṛṣṇa, Kṛṣṇa eventually reveals Himself as the Supreme Personality.

We're very fortunate to have had contact with Śrīla Prabhupāda, who is very dear to Kṛṣṇa and who has told us about pure devotional service. If we take up devotional service, Prabhupāda assures us we can have our own individual relationship with Kṛṣṇa. Kṛṣṇa is always with His pure associates. Our own *gurudeva* is surely one of those associates and the one whom we want to follow to please Kṛṣṇa. When someone asks me how we can think of Kṛṣṇa, I say we should hear as much as we can from the *rasa-śāstras* about Kṛṣṇa in Vṛndāvana, how Kṛṣṇa is happy, and what He is really like. Then we will naturally start thinking about Him. And we should chant His holy name. We should chant as well as hear and think about Kṛṣṇa.

Kṛṣṇa sometimes sends persons who are eternally participating in His pastimes, and they tell us what it is like to be with Kṛṣṇa. They share their visions and even their devotions. For example, Śrīla Vyāsadeva, the great sage who compiled the *Vedas*, is actually Kṛṣṇa in His literary incarnation. By studying the *Vedas*, we receive the actual revelation of God's form and pastimes. Just so we know what devotional service is, Kṛṣṇa came as His own devotee in the form of Lord Caitanya. All the inner moods of devotion are recounted in *Caitanya-caritāmṛta*. If we want to think about Kṛṣṇa, we may read *Caitanya-caritāmṛta* and *Kṛṣṇa* book and think about what is written there. True, devotional life is not all found in books. As Prabhupāda himself says, book knowledge is theoretical; Deity worship is practical. Descriptions of Kṛṣṇa in Vṛndāvana are not theory, but for us, Kṛṣṇa's pastimes are something we can only read in books. Yet if we read *śāstra* submissively, we can enter the spiritual world through its pages; they are not ordinary books.

Until we come to the stage of spontaneous attraction to Kṛṣṇa, we have to use our bodies and minds in Kṛṣṇa's service. That is what Prabhupāda means by practical service. In Deity worship there are so many practical considerations, such as cooking for Kṛṣṇa, dressing Kṛṣṇa, bathing Kṛṣṇa. These activities focus our lives on Kṛṣṇa. By vibrating Kṛṣṇa's name, serving Kṛṣṇa, and remembering Kṛṣṇa's pastimes, our whole life becomes absorbed in remembrance of Kṛṣṇa.

Prabhupāda has given us the open secret to preach Kṛṣṇa consciousness to others as a way of pleasing Kṛṣṇa. And when we please Kṛṣṇa, He will reveal Himself more and more. Because we're followers of Prabhupāda, we can never become too delinquent in telling others about Kṛṣṇa. Prabhupāda will remind us.

I think talking about this should be an integral part of our relationship. In honoring the best in each of us and honoring our desire to serve Prabhupāda, we can ask each other, "How are you doing?" Do you know that famous question King Daśaratha asked the sage Viśvāmitra when they met—*aihiṣṭaṁ yat tat punar-janma-jayāya*, is everything going well in your endeavor to conquer the repetition of birth and death? The king asked Viśvāmitra that because he knew it was the sage's concern. Just as you would ask a businessman, "How's business?" Or a mother, "How are your children?" so you ask a Kṛṣṇa conscious person how he is doing in his attempt to overcome repeated birth and death. And you would ask a devotee of Prabhupāda, "How are you doing in your attempt to serve the *saṅkīrtana* movement?"

This question is raised between us not in an accusing way to make us feel guilty. We can answer honestly, knowing that we love each other. I know you're trying to do something. So you say, "Well I haven't been doing so well lately," but then you share with me some activity you are doing. Maybe it's small and you're a little bashful about it, but it is something that gives you pleasure, someone you're cultivating, or an instance when you were able to speak about Kṛṣṇa. And I can encourage you. Then you can inquire how I'm doing. This will help us because we take pleasure by imbibing Kṛṣṇa consciousness and distributing it.

July 26
Wicklow

Dear friends,

I started on my walk this morning with umbrella in hand, hood up, boots on. I was on the lookout for animals. I looked at the trees and thought of them as friends. Then I tried to cast my thoughts to Vṛndāvana-dhāma, but the umbrella caught in the wind and tugged at my hand as if to remind me that I'm in Ireland, not in Vraja. I can't expect to get out easily. At least I'm not a householder with lots of cares and responsibilities. Kṛṣṇa has freed me. But freed me to do what? To serve Kṛṣṇa and tell others about Him.

I'm getting the feeling that my time here at Wicklow is running out, both in terms of letters and morning walks, and that I ought to begin winding it up. It's good that it's ending. We're walking over the same ground repeatedly.

Of course, it can be good to be familiar with a place and to have a familiar solitude. But I think I'm getting ready to go to Vṛndāvana. There the ground is special. But even if I were to stay and continue to walk this road, it would be possible to go further into Kṛṣṇa consciousness. In order to do that I would have to get Kṛṣṇa's mercy and I would have to find new paths, not necessarily new paths in a material sense, but new paths within, new approaches to Kṛṣṇa.

For example, in past visits to Ireland at this time of year, I would pray as I walked early in the morning. I had been reading about prayer in the Christian tradition and was trying to enter the life of prayer. Now I'm in quite a different mood. I hope in the future I will be moving down the road of *bhakti,* closer to seeing the dust of Vṛndāvana wherever I am.

I wish I could improve my *japa,* but something is preventing me. It seems strange that there are offenses that we've committed that we're not sharply aware of when we chant. If you had a thorn or pebble in your shoe, you would feel it as you walked; you know what's causing the impediment and can do something about it. But if I'm offending Vaiṣṇavas and then I go to chant, the impediment it causes is not so clear. It's subtle. My inattention is clear, but it's mostly out of my control. I can't even see why I'm inattentive, although I accept Bhaktivinoda Ṭhākura's analysis that it's due to attraction to worldly things. That's almost a definition of inattention. But I guess my question is, "Why can't my desire for good chanting overcome my interest in worldly things?" I don't know the answer to that question, except again in a theoretical way—that my desire is simply not strong enough. That's all. That's an answer, but one that only defines my regrettable situation.

Why not discuss this basic inattention and this lack of desire which prevents me from hearing the holy name? I can't even cry out, "Kṛṣṇa, please let me hear You." Of course, if one chants loudly, the very utterances of the syllables of the Hare Kṛṣṇa mantra become a way to cry out and express emotion. Just as with loud shouting you can chase away a bear, so you can likewise try to banish inattention. But sometimes if one continues to chant loudly, it becomes a vociferous bellowing without the delicate feeling of serving and loving Kṛṣṇa. So whether it's yelling or whispering, whether it's attentive or inattentive—any kind of utterance of the holy names is within Kṛṣṇa consciousness. We can think of it as many concentric circles drawn with a compass, a bull's eye. All utterances of the holy names are within some circle, but usually they're in the outer circles. Hare Kṛṣṇa Hare Kṛṣṇa, Kṛṣṇa Kṛṣṇa Hare Hare/Hare Rāma Hare Rāma, Rāma Rāma Hare Hare. Who is chanting thoughtfully? Who is trying to hit closer to the bull's eye? Are we just haphazardly scattering mantras? Hare Kṛṣṇa. Hare Kṛṣṇa.

Kṛṣṇa, please accept this prayer which isn't wholehearted, but which I nonetheless offer. Please help me pay attention. Give me the strength to do rigorous practice, even if it seems an austerity to hear again and again the sound of the mantra, so that eventually I may remember that this is Kṛṣṇa, the person, and that I may make gains in *harināma-bhajana*.

The holy name is always inviting us to chant again. I lament as in Lord Caitanya's verse, that I don't taste the wonderful nectar that Kṛṣṇa assures us is available in His name. But I do taste something. There's something tantalizing me to go forward with faith. It's faith, but also experience. And now we're gaining knowledge that there's so much more we have to put into the chanting, so much more we can realize from the chanting. We want to understand that from the names comes Kṛṣṇa's form, qualities, and pastimes. We want to practice in that way. O holy name, You alone can grant benediction to the living beings. Therefore the Lord has hundreds and thousands of names. But we are most interested in His names Kṛṣṇa and Govinda, which speak of His pastimes in Vṛndāvana-*dhāma* among His cows and cowherd friends.

July 27
Wicklow

Dear friends,

It's colder this morning than perhaps ever before. The wind is blowing dark blue-gray clouds across a light blue sky. At the end of the uphill road I saw lights coming from the schoolhouse. The evergreens on both sides were dark and dense. It was like a painting by Van Gogh—that little house at the top of the rise and then beyond it, the hills. This morning the sliver moon hung like a cradle. Dear friends, your humble correspondent is glad to be here and to be talking to you via this long distance connection. I say humble correspondent because he's feeling humbled by an inability to do the best thing in Kṛṣṇa consciousness, to be completely śāstric. And he's humbled by seeing that he is egotistical. It stings to say that and stings more when others say it. I know the remedy and I'm taking it, but to others, the remedy looks like more egotism. I'm referring to my writing, even this letter-writing. So I sting and smart because I know it's true that I indulge in self-centeredness, but I don't see a better remedy.

How beautiful this morning is. So quiet and lovely. And so cold that my fingers become stiff. Who could complain? Such a beautiful mood. And the trees, like sentinels, standing watch so quietly. It's overwhelming. But it's Kṛṣṇa. It's Kṛṣṇa. We don't forget.

Then came the little scene that is repeated every weekday. As I approached the schoolhouse,

I saw Prabhupāda dāsa leaning against the window. He was actually looking for me to come by. As soon as he thinks I see him, he ducks away. But I always see him first. I know because he remains there a while before he ducks out of sight. I don't wave. He's so nice and shy that he would be embarrassed if I waved and, so to speak, caught him there. At one point he pulls back from the window and I round the bend and walk in the opposite direction (I still don't know if it is north or south).

And so dear friend, what shall we have today for philosophy, for our pre-breakfast feast? What shall we discuss? For breakfast *prasādam* I like the same thing everyday. I'd rather Madhu not vary it. Let me have several kinds of fruit and yogurt—that's all. So maybe we can return to some of our favorite topics, but bring to them an attitude that is fresh and sincere. For instance, seeing Kṛṣṇa in material nature—how can we do it in a way pleasing to Kṛṣṇa? How can we remember the *rasa* of Kṛṣṇa's pastimes even while we see the moon go behind clouds and reemerge or a fox run across our path?

We think of the physician Mukunda who saw a peacock fan being waved by an attendant of the Muslim king. He fainted and fell off a high platform. The Muslim king could understand that Mukunda was actually experiencing love of God. So that's a topic, isn't it? A topic that is very important to us. Does Kṛṣṇa really want us to see this place as void and not appreciate its richness? If we see the morning sights with intense pleasure, does that mean we're going to suffer intensely also? Is this an attachment to the world?

July 28
Wicklow, Ireland

Dear friends,

It's a clear morning; hardly a cloud to be seen. A jet passing overhead has left a white trail across the sky. An unusual sight in Wicklow. It is so nice and quiet here, only the sounds of birds waking up. So maybe we'll have some clear talk, if there is some connection between the weather and my viewpoint.

On a clear day you can see for great distances. So one would hope to see more Kṛṣṇa consciousness. However, if a full moon is auspicious for thinking, we have just the opposite—the faintest sliver is all that's left in this morning's sky. Kṛṣṇa has been painting His magnificent sky vistas. There looks to be a thumb print in the clouds, and the way the clouds are shifting suggests that someone has just moved. Kṛṣṇa's artistry has a personal quality.

When we speak of clarity, we mean the ability of the *jīva* to see not only clear cloudless skies, but also his *anarthas*. If you can see your own *anarthas* you can hope to remove them. The example is given that a dark spot on a white cloth is prominent and spoils the cloth, but if the spot is removed, the white cloth will be nice again. Another image comes to mind of a person who has a facial mole or birthmark. A disfiguring birthmark is easily enough noticed, but not so easily removed. But the ugliness of our *anarthas* is not like that. Rather, the blemish of our *anarthas* is just asking to be removed. The soul wants to be free of defects in order to love and serve Kṛṣṇa. Kṛṣṇa Himself wants the *anarthas* removed. Sometimes we even translate *anartha* as "unwanted thing." But how are our *anarthas* to be eliminated?

In this beautiful clear dawn with pink coming up and everywhere a changing vista, you begin to think Kṛṣṇa is so beautiful. Maybe the *anarthas* get washed out. Maybe it could be compared to washing a speck of dirt out of your eye.

As I watched the unblemished landscape, a big badger appeared on the scene and startled me. He brought me back to earth, such an earthly fellow. I stamped my feet out of fear and annoyance that my train of thought had been broken. At first he kept coming toward me, but then he started off in the other direction, a bit peeved perhaps that he should have to cede his turf to a man who stamps his foot. But this is clarity too, isn't it? Seeing what's actually there, seeing the badger, seeing one's own fear, seeing the ethereal nature of one's thoughts? Where's the rhapsodic harmony now?

This morning the badger interrupted my reverie, but it didn't negate my point: when we become filled with the beauty of Kṛṣṇa, our *anarthas* will go away. But the badger's intrusion can be taken to mean that enlightenment has to be grounded in practicality too. Otherwise, we may think we are liberated just because we feel a moment's exaltation. Sometimes even in the name of ecstasy we can make mistakes, and what is taken for clarity turns out to be illusion. Still, the more we can be filled with the realization of Kṛṣṇa, false exaltation will fade away.

When things become clear, what do you see? You begin to see Kṛṣṇa with His bluish complexion, standing by the Vaṁśīvaṭa playing His flute. The *gopīs* and all the creatures fortunate enough to hear it become enchanted by the sound. You see Kṛṣṇa and His cowherd friends. You see Kṛṣṇa with the *gopīs*. This is what you see when things become clear. And this is the benediction Bhīṣmadeva asked of Kṛṣṇa at the end of his life: let me see Kṛṣṇa coming toward me on the battlefield. Let me see Kṛṣṇa in His different pastimes. That which now seems like *śāstra* or theology becomes our actual field of vision. This is real seeing. Everything else is mist.

My morning walk was interrupted a second time. As I walked back I began to hear a tiny meowing. I looked up thinking it was some kind of cat-bird. Then along the wall I saw a tiny gray kitten crying pitifully. It came toward me and wanted me to take care of it. We've all had an encounter with a kitten in the wild who runs to us, wanting to be saved. I kept walking to get away from it, and as I walked, I recalled stories about how sages should not get attached to animals. Gradually the sound faded, but then it became stronger again and I looked back. There was the kitten running toward me. It was so pitifully seeking shelter. I paused for just a second and it ran faster, but then I turned and kept walking. What could I do for the creature? I'm not going to take it home for a pet. In this way we sometimes have to turn our back on pitiful cries and get on with the business of making ourselves fit in Kṛṣṇa consciousness so that we can truly help people. Otherwise, we ourselves become like pitiful kittens when we go to lecture or guide others. I say this, but still I stop on the road and look back. Where is the kitty?

July 29
Wicklow

Dear friends,

I can feel that I'm coming to the end of this correspondence with you. I leave Wicklow in a few days and my mind is turning to something else. Although I'll be able to write my usual correspondence (I was almost going to say my "official" correspondence), I may have to stop these letters from a *sannyāsī* for a while.

It's been fun writing them. At first I was confused about whom to write, but since coming to Wicklow I have done best by settling on you, my friends. I've tried to speak from the heart and tell you what was happening with me. In these letters to you I can speak whatever I have to say on a particular day and you won't hold it against me if it isn't wholehearted or from the core of my being. You will accept that it was at least all I had on a particular day, and rather than be sealed off alone, I could share with you even my little attempts in Kṛṣṇa consciousness. So perhaps that's a definition of heart-to-heart talks; they are sincere expressions.

I can see that I'm coming to the end, coming out of the deep feelings of the Wicklow walks. They have been very nice. Probably if I had to stay I could return to the mood of these walks. I haven't exhausted what I could find here. But because I know I have to go, my mind is trying to leave a few days before my actual departure. I do that to ease the pain of separation.

I was thinking more about how friends come together in Kṛṣṇa consciousness. We have faith that our friendship isn't a temporary coming together, but is based on eternal *rasa* with Kṛṣṇa. While we can't perceive this we acknowledge that we have the same spiritual masters, that the most important thing in life is God consciousness, and that we have a very close understanding that Kṛṣṇa is the Supreme Personality of Godhead and His activities in Kṛṣṇaloka constitute the highest and most intimate form of love and existence. It's a shame that people who agree on these things sometimes quarrel. We hear that personalities in the spiritual world have differences, but the differences are without malice. Here, I guess it's also mostly without malice, but it's disappointing when differences arise. When we can find friendships, therefore, we should invest in them and work on them so they don't become inhibited. And even those relationships that don't seem to work so wonderfully should be protected against *vaiṣṇava aparādha*.

For the first time on the walk today, after three weeks, I heard a dog bark from a farmhouse. Maybe that's another signal that my time is coming to an end. Even then the barking was not so bad. The dog was distant and did not become maniacal. As you can see, I don't have anything new or brilliant to say, and I hope you agree that it isn't necessary. What's necessary is a kind of mutual concern so that when our friend speaks, we listen and think how to apply it to Kṛṣṇa consciousness. In that way, we open to another voice, another mind, and that sharing enriches our experience. A friend may say, "It's important to pay attention and try to pray while you're chanting." One could say these are ordinary words. But still, if we hear them carefully and submissively, not always in the guru-disciple relationship but in a mood of friendship, the advice our friend gives can spark off our own Kṛṣṇa consciousness.

I'm speaking of friendship. But I'm reminded of an inferior relationship as illustrated by yesterday's encounter with the kitten. The kitten looked to me as its savior.

As I walked on the road today the kitten again appeared making her pitiful cries. She wanted me to help her. When we came close to each other I looked to see if she was starving. She didn't look that bad, but she was abandoned. And then I made the mistake of stopping. Before I knew it she was under my feet. That rather frightened me because I didn't know she was there and I kicked to get her away and even had to start running to get away, but she just kept coming and crying and crying. I didn't want to tell you this ridiculous tale. I don't know exactly what it means. But it's very unattractive for a *sannyāsī* to be approached by a pitiful, dependent kitten.

In Kṛṣṇa consciousness I hope I'm not like that, and that we can give and take in an exchange that is mutually beneficial to our Kṛṣṇa consciousness. When you see me on the road, I hope you don't cry or cringe, thinking me to be your savior. We can't do that for each other; only Kṛṣṇa can save us. There are cases when people have to maintain others materially, but I'm not talking about that. I'm talking about voluntary friendships given to each other.

I wasn't too happy about acting in that way, and I can't quite say who will take care of the starving kittens and the starving people of the world. Are we not to raise a finger in any way? We don't want whimpering friends, but there are whimpering entities. Who is going to take care of them? It's a reminder of the whole world situation. Faced with the different problems of the world and different attitudes toward these problems, we're taking the path given by our spiritual master to try to give Kṛṣṇa consciousness to everyone. Its benediction will filter down to all living entities.

But immediately I think about the kitten. Why respond to the kitten just because it's crying? Why not bring home a cow or a calf? They're just sitting there; they don't make any protest, like the kitten. I have all kinds of rationalizations, but still the kitten has sought my help. Maybe it's a superstition, but I sometimes think that God may be manifesting Himself to me in every ordinary encounter. Just like the demigods who would sometimes come in the form of dogs, even pigeons, to test the generosity of the king. Maybe my heart is being tested.

Anyway, when I got to the end of the road, I thought about it before starting back. Was I going to just kick the kitten away or run past it? I decided to pick it up and bring it to the schoolhouse. Maybe our veterinarian friend, Abhaya dāsī, could find a home for it. It would be icky-sticky to pick up the kitten. I haven't done something like that in awhile, but I could carry it for a few minutes.

So I'll tell you what happened. As I walked back, sure enough the gray kitten was there crying, so I let her come up to me and I thought she was well formed, a gray tabby with many colors. I picked her up and carried her a while, petting her and reassuring her, but then she wanted down. So I let her down and she again came to me. I picked her up again. I was resolved to bring her to the schoolhouse, but again she got wriggly and wanted down. So at this point I let her down and kept walking without thinking much about it. This time she did not make a desperate attempt to follow me. I guess you would say that I satisfied myself that we really didn't have that much to do together and that I wasn't bound to carry her and coerce her to come with me. She was a creature of the wild somehow and there was nothing I could really do, although I had made the gesture.

You could say I wasn't determined and that's a fact. I haven't been trained to take this as a very important thing to do and I had already neglected my rounds. I was willing to forego that, but then she resisted so much I lost my determination. If nothing else, I want this experience to remind me that I have to be determined to be kindhearted with my fellow beings, humans especially, because they are meant for receiving Kṛṣṇa consciousness.

Maybe I'm not so determined with human beings either, and only when I can carry somebody who is a little quiet and doesn't wriggle away will I persist. But let me take it as a kind of failure in saintly compassion that I didn't stick with this kitten, and let me try to make up for it by sticking with the devotees as much as I can in the course of my own Kṛṣṇa consciousness.

Acknowledgements

I would like to thank the following disciples and friends for helping to produce and print this book: Nāndīmukhī-devī dāsī, Mādhava dāsa, Kaiśorī-devī dāsī, Caitanya-rūpa-devī dāsī, Lālitāmṛta-devī dāsī, Keśihanta dāsa, Guru-sevā-devī dāsī (drawings), Hare Kṛṣṇa dāsī (cover artwork), Madana-mohana dāsa (cover design), and Bhaktin Cindy Min.